MW00780619

Historical and Contemporary Foundations of Social Studies Education

This book explores the rich history and depth of the educational field of social studies in the United States and examines its capacity to moderate modern-day anti-democratic forces through a commitment to civic education.

Drawing out key significant historical moments within the development of social studies education, it provides a compelling historical narrative of the ideas that shaped the unique curricular field of social studies education. This book resynthesizes each historical stage to show how it resonates with contemporary life and effectively helps readers bridge the gap between theory and practice. Focusing on the key ideas of the field and the primary individuals who championed those ideas, the author provides a clear, concise, and sharply pointed encounter with social studies education that illuminates the connection from research to practice.

Researchers of social studies education will find this book to be a worthy contribution to the ever-important struggle to better understand the type of civic education necessary for the perpetuation of democratic life in the United States. It will also appeal to educational researchers and teacher educators with interests in the history of education, teacher education, civic education, moral education, and democracy.

James E. Schul is a professor in the Department of Education Studies at Winona State University, USA. He is the author of *Paradoxes of the Public School: Historical and Contemporary Foundations of American Public Education*, named in 2020 as an Outstanding Academic Title by Choice Reviews.

Routledge Research in Character and Virtue Education

This series provides a forum for established and emerging scholars to discuss the latest debates, research and theory relating to virtue education, character education and value education.

For more information about this series, please visit: www.routledge.com/Routledge-Research-in-Character-and-Virtue-Education/book-series/RRCVE

Historical and Contemporary Foundations of Social Studies Education

Unpacking Implications for Civic Education and Contemporary Life

James E. Schul

Routledge
Taylor & Francis Group

NEW YORK AND LONDON

First published 2023
by Routledge
605 Third Avenue, New York, NY 10158

and by Routledge
4 Park Square, Milton Park, Abingdon, Oxon, OX14 4RN

Routledge is an imprint of the Taylor & Francis Group, an informa business

© 2023 James E. Schul

ISBN: 978-1-032-44299-0 (hbk)
ISBN: 978-1-032-44468-0 (pbk)
ISBN: 978-1-003-37231-8 (ebk)

DOI: 10.4324/9781003372318

Typeset in Times New Roman
by Apex CoVantage, LLC

To Christa.

Contents

Acknowledgements

This book emerged out of a culmination of many people investing their time and energy into me and my development.

I will always be grateful to Mike Fuller who believed in me and advocated for me.

While at the University of Iowa, I was fortunate to be guided by an outstanding group of scholars: Bruce Fehn, Peter Hlebowitsh, Greg Hamot, Kathy Schuh, and Christine Ogren. This book first emerged in my mind while in Greg Hamot's graduate seminar on social studies education. Greg's passion for democratic citizenship and the key figures in the history of social studies education spilled over into me.

I am grateful for my professional relationships across the country. In particular, my involvement in the Society for the Study of Curriculum History has been an invaluable resource for my growth. A special thanks to the editorial team at Routledge, especially Alice Salt, who believed in this book.

I am fortunate to be the father of four wonderful children: Lani, Wilt, Swin, and Myrene. They enrich my life.

This book is dedicated to my spouse, Christa. My career in academia was made possible by her. I live a life rich in love and support thanks to her.

Introduction

Liberty cannot be preserved without a general knowledge among the people, who have a right . . . and a desire to know; but besides this, they have a right, an indisputable, unalienable, indefeasible, divine right to that most dreaded and envied kind of knowledge, I mean of the characters and conduct of their rulers.

– John Adams (1765)

The United States of America was born in the late eighteenth century as an experiment in liberal democracy. Rising in the wake of the European enlightenment, the founders of the United States boldly risked putting into reality a country bound together through a social contract between the people and their government. This social contract was conceived in a series of "self-evident truths" clearly articulated in the United States' Declaration of Independence of 1776:

- "All men are created equal."
- "That they are endowed by their Creator with certain unalienable Rights, that among these are Life, Liberty and the pursuit of Happiness."
- "That to secure these rights, Governments are instituted among Men, deriving their just powers from the consent of the governed."
- "That whenever any Form of Government becomes destructive of these ends, it is the Right of the People to alter or to abolish it, and to institute new Government, laying its foundation on such principles and organizing its powers in such form, as to them shall seem most likely to effect their Safety and Happiness."
- "Prudence, indeed, will dictate that Governments long established should not be changed for light and transient causes; and accordingly all experience hath shewn, that mankind are more disposed to suffer, while evils are sufferable, than to right themselves by abolishing the forms to which they are accustomed."

These are, arguably, perfect propositions for an imperfect union of states to be dedicated to. This dedication, however, is no easy matter. It requires intentional work. The constitutional codification of the country was a necessary and central piece of this intentional work. Yet much of this work required institutional support as well. A pivotal moment for the sustenance of the country's liberal democracy came with the emergence of the common public school in the nineteenth century. It became the country's first social network intentionally designed to support its liberal democracy. The next step was taken in the early twentieth century with the advent of social studies education as a curricular field within the school system specifically dedicated to cultivating liberal democracy into perpetuity.

Historical and Contemporary Foundations of Social Studies Education tells the story of significant historical moments within social studies education and shapes each historical stage of this story to address how it resonates with contemporary life. Focusing on the key ideas of the field and the primary individuals who championed those ideas, this book provides the clear, concise, and sharply pointed encounter with social studies education that all educational researchers will find provocative and inspiring while possessing a crossover appeal to teacher educators who aspire to put this research into practice. Researchers of social studies education will find this book to be a worthy contribution to the ever-important struggle to better understand the type of civic education necessary for the perpetuation of democratic life in the United States.

John Dewey famously said in his 1916 book *Democracy and Education* that "the past is the history of the present." This is certainly true about the field of social studies education. Consider the following questions:

- Should teachers impose their political beliefs upon students?
- How might individuals better discern information they consume?
- How should history be taught to cultivate democratic citizenship?
- How might teachers address controversial issues in their classroom?
- How may a teacher develop morality among students?

These questions are certainly relevant for contemporary times. Yet these questions were raised at a much earlier time by scholarly individuals who approached them carefully, and articulately contributed their ideas to enrich and expand the broad field of social studies education.

What you are about to read emerged out of my desire to create a book that I needed to read when I was an undergraduate learning to be a social studies teacher. I merge the past and present with the hope that it propels education for democratic citizenship forward. Unfortunately, social studies teachers are seldom exposed to the rich history of the field they belong to. Such exposure usually occurs at the graduate level and in a particular graduate-level program dedicated to social studies education. Not all teachers have such opportunity. This isn't to say that there haven't been excellent things written about the field of social studies education. Without the excellent historical scholarship of Hazel Hertzberg, Ronald Evans, and Walter Parker, for instance, this book would, frankly, not be possible. Yet I never could find a singular source that succinctly wove together the historical and contemporary foundations of social studies education together in a way that practically addressed the realities of teachers, students, and the classrooms they cohabitate.

The chapters are arranged in chronological order of what I believe to be the advent of movements or seminal work by scholars in the field. However, this chronology is imprecise due to the overlapping of some of these occurrences. The career of Harold Rugg, alone, for instance, encompassed nearly three decades. So the chronology may be fodder for discussion among some of you – but the arrangement of the chapters was my decision and how I see the evolvement of the field. Table I.1 represents a chronological outline of the chapters within this book:

Historically speaking, Chapter 1 focuses on the creation of social studies education in 1916. Chapters 2 and 3 address social reconstructionism and propaganda education, both of which were most prominent in the 1930s, respectively. Chapter 4 features the notable work from the 1940s of Alan Griffin regarding identifying how history teaching for democratic citizenship should look. The 1940s was also a time where the controversy surrounding Harold Rugg's textbooks began to take hold across the socio-political landscape of the United States. It is that signifying turning point in the field where I look at the issue in Chapter 5 of addressing social problems in the classroom. Chapters 6–9 address various issues that surfaced throughout the 1960s to the 1990s. These issues include Maurice Hunt and Lawrence Metcalf's emphasis on addressing closed areas in the classroom (Chapter 6), the new social studies movement and the rise of historical thinking (Chapter 7), the work of Lawrence Kohlberg and Nel Noddings with regard to

Table I.1 Chronological Outline of *Historical and Contemporary Foundations of Social Studies Education*

1910s	1930s	1940s	1960s–1990s	Contemporary Times
Chapter 1	Chapter 2	Chapter 4	Chapter 6	Chapter 10
	Chapter 3	Chapter 5	Chapter 7	
			Chapter 8	
			Chapter 9	

moral education (Chapter 8), and the reclamation efforts of Shirley Engle to bring citizenship education at front and center of social studies education (Chapter 9). Finally, Chapter 10 emphasized the three fused curricular areas of global education, multiculturalism, and technology education that all significantly surfaced in the late twentieth century but currently play a significant role in the contemporary landscape of the field.

While a chronological history is the basis for the arrangement of the chapters, each chapter emphasizes a contemporary issue related to that historical theme. In this sense, this book is arranged through a social melioristic lens. In this spirit of social meliorism and my dire concern that this book be a practical contributor to classroom practice, each chapter begins with a fictional vignette that focuses on the chapter's particular theme in one way or another. These vignettes feature the fictional character of Madi Hobbs, a first-year social studies teacher. You will learn much more about Madi as you read this book. It is my hope that you and other readers can relate with her and the school environment where she works.

It is my sincere hope that you enjoy reading this book as much as I enjoyed writing it. Whether you are a burgeoning educational researcher, teacher educator, or practicing teacher, I wrote it with your interest in mind. I also wrote it with a sense of optimism that prioritizing the field of social studies education will blossom a bright future for democratic life. Our democracy will not magically survive with wishful spectatorship and pixie dust. Instead, it needs careful curricular cultivation and a willingness by us to roll up our sleeves and go about the work of civic education. The present and future of our democratic life depends upon what goes in our social studies classroom. So, let's get to work!

1 American Invention

The early summer sunrise signaled a new dawn for Middleborough High School. The previous week was filled with workshops and new faculty orientation. On this Monday, however, the adolescent-aged residents of Middleborough trekked to their high school for the very first time after a summer of work, play, and an acquaintance with later nights and mornings. Some arrived on the large yellow buses while some upperclassmen came driving used cars new to them. As they noisily flooded through the front door, each went their own way. For those who strolled to room 212, a fresh face greeted them.

Madeline ("Madi") Elizabeth Hobbs was fresh out of college and was told in her interview that she had big shoes to fill. Mr. Perry retired after 38 years of teaching high school social studies. By all accounts, students and teachers adored him. But none of that mattered to Madi because she was not part of that past. The present was on her mind, and the young men and women who took seats in her classroom were now her responsibility.

She was up to the task. Her parents blessed her with a combination of a blue-collar work ethic and a passion for the life of the mind. Her biggest influence from college, Dr. Ellsworth, insisted that all social studies teachers keep things relevant. He insisted on excellence and took social studies education seriously. "If you can't connect your lesson to today," he commonly exclaimed, "then you shouldn't be teaching it!" She was ready to put those words into practice as she looked upon her first class for the first time.

We usually think of inventions as material objects akin to why Benjamin Franklin, Thomas Edison, or Steve Jobs are famously known. In the world of education, however, it is feasible for an educational field to be invented and live a life of its own. This is exactly what happened with social studies education. Madi Hobbs was a newly minted member of a field uniquely created in the United States to serve a socio-civic purpose. Social studies education and the United States of America are intrinsically intertwined with one another. The specific purpose of social studies education is to support

DOI:10.4324/9781003372318-1

the American democratic project where the government derives its power "from the consent of the governed." In this chapter, we will explore the origins of social studies education, its purpose, and what it was intended to look like. In doing this, we will examine the philosophical underpinnings behind social studies education as well as examine the significant role that John Dewey played in its creation and development. We then close with the role public school teachers played with the success, or lack thereof, of social studies education and how the field's future remains intertwined with the ability of teachers to fulfill its ambitious civic purpose.

The 1916 Report

The world was torn apart by the second decade of the twentieth century. Engulfed in a global conflict unparalleled at the time, many nations in the world sought a path toward healing and peace. The United States of America shared this desire for a better world. Although the US did not enter what was then called "The Great War" (now called World War I in the wake of its sad sequel two decades later) until 1917, the spirit behind its entry had been brewing for quite some time. President Woodrow Wilson was a byproduct of the hopeful period historians call "the progressive era," and his eventual push for entry into the war was guided by a fervent belief the war would become "the war to end all wars." The progressive movement was a complex era in US history consisting of economic, political, educational, and social reform efforts that sometimes seemed at odds with one another other. At the thrust of these reform efforts was a sense of optimism that society could be dramatically improved with human intervention. This is the contextual backdrop for the creation of social studies education.

The year 1916 holds special distinction for social studies education. In that year, the National Education Association's (NEA) *Commission on the Reorganization of Secondary Education* (CRSE) published its *Report of the Social Studies*.[1] It sprouted from the CRSE's Committee on the Social Studies (CSS), a subcommittee formed in 1913 by the CRSE. In its 1916 report, the CSS used, for the first official time, the phrase "social studies" to describe the collective curriculum of the history and the social sciences in the secondary curriculum. The report was part of a larger effort among educational professionals and academics to modernize the secondary school curriculum to meet the changing needs of society such as curricular relevancy, an emphasis on current issues, and the fostering of interdependence as opposed to rugged individualism. Such features were hallmark characteristics of education initiatives at the time of World War I (Fallace, 2008).

The CSS consisted of 21 members. The membership consisted mostly of educators (i.e., school principals and education professors) but was significantly influenced by historian *James Harvey Robinson* (1863–1936). Robinson, employed by Columbia University while he served on the CSS, was a leading figure in the New History movement that emerged in the field of history. The New History movement perceived history as having significant power in addressing contemporary issues. This paradigm on the role of history ran perfectly parallel with the views of Robinson's most celebrated colleague, philosopher *John Dewey* (1859–1952). While not a member of the CSS, Dewey was arguably its most significant influence. We will examine Dewey and the ideas he shared with Robinson later in this chapter to help us better understand the influences behind the 1916 Report.

The 1916 Report is approximately 100 pages long but holds enormous influence. According to social studies educator Shirley Engle (1994), it "is widely believed to be the most important document in the long history of citizenship education in this country" and it "legitimated the term 'social studies' to designate formal citizenship education and placed squarely in the field of those subjects that were believed to contribute to that end" (p. vii). Table 1.1 displays a synopsis of the report. Three key components exist within the report: the definition of social studies, a proposed course outline, and a proposed pedagogical approach to subject matter. The remainder of this section will closely examine each of these three components.

The first key component of the report is that it provided a definition for social studies education. This definition tied the field directly to the "organization and development of human society" and individuals "as a member of societal groups" (Nelson, 1994, p. 9). Rather than focusing on a form of

Table 1.1 Synopsis of 1916 NEA Report on the Social Studies in Secondary Education (Nelson, 1994)

Definition of Social Studies:
"… those whose subject matter relates directly to the organization and development of human society, and to man as a member of societal groups (p. 9)

Proposed Course Outline	*Proposed Pedagogical Approach to Subject Matter:*
Junior years (grades 7–9): Geography European history American history Civics Senior years (grades 10–12): European history American history Problems of democracy – social, economic, and political (p. 11)	(1) The adoption to the fullest extent possible of a "topical" method or a "problem" method, as opposed to a method based on chronological sequence alone. (2) The selection of topics or problems for students with reference to (a) the pupil's own immediate interest and (b) general social significance (p. 35).

individual development, the report's definition placed the development of a good society central to the field. This directly tied social studies education to democratic citizenship, without using those explicit words. Second, the report proposed a course outline for both grades 7–9 and then grades 10–12. This outline kept intact a separation of social science disciplines (i.e., geography, European history, American history) that already existed in the school curriculum. There were two exceptions, however, where the report recommended two amalgamated courses: civics and problems of democracy. Finally, and perhaps most significantly, the report proposed a particular approach teachers should use to teach subject matter. This proposed pedagogical approach posited that teachers should teach history topically or with a central problem to be addressed as opposed to using chronology to drive lessons. This approach also suggested that teachers prioritize the direct interests of students and societal significance when considering what and how a particular piece of subject matter should be taught. This latter component of a preferred pedagogical approach was clearly influenced by tendencies of its members, particularly James Harvey Robinson, to adhere to social meliorism. It is with this point that the influence of John Dewey on the CSS was most apparent.

Dewey and Social Meliorism

Social meliorism is a philosophy that optimistically emphasizes the importance of human intervention to improve society from its unfavorable natural tendencies. In sum, meliorists believe that society can improve with the intelligent help of people. It is rooted in the ideals of American *pragmatism* from the turn of the twentieth century that stipulated the worthiness of ideas depended upon their practical application. According to pragmatic thinking, society's improvement depended upon humanity's willingness to engage in reflective inquiry and problem solving. This diverts from any form of ideological thinking that posits that ideas are worthwhile if they fit a perceived blueprint on how society should work. As a result, pragmatism runs against the grain of ideological thinking and a reliance on conventional trends. The best solution to a problem, according to pragmatism, emerges from individuals' deliberate and reflective inquiry – even if that solution diverts from previous practice.

The idea that humans can alter the natural course of events through problem solving that emanates from deliberation and reflection is a significant trademark of the progressive education movement that flourished most prominently at the turn of the twentieth century. The progressive education movement consisted of a series of reform efforts that, though at times deeply contrasted with each other, all sought to improve the public school experience in the United States (Tyack, 1974). The reform effort from the progressive era we will focus on in this chapter is the one focused on pedagogy, or the teaching and learning of youth. Historian David Tyack (1974) called advocates of this reform effort the pedagogical progressives. The pedagogical progressives were influenced by the growing interest in childhood that infiltrated Western civilization in the latter half of the nineteenth century (Reese, 2001). Out of this influence emerged several prominent reformers, most notably *Maria Montessori* (1870–1952) and *Friedrich Froebel* (1782–1852), who each designed teaching and learning strategies designed to cater to the interests and predilections of children. The conversations among the progressives took a significant turn at the turn of the twentieth century through the efforts of several reformers who sought to make a stronger connection between the child's nature and the democratic aims of society. There are numerous progressive educators who were counted among this group such as *Boyd Bode* (1873–1953), *William Kilpatrick* (1871–1965), *Ernest Horn* (1882–1967), and *Alexander James Inglis* (1879–1924). However, no reformer was as prolific or influential in perpetuating this new type of progressive education than John Dewey.

Dewey was a philosopher who, along with *Charles Peirce* (1839–1914), *William James* (1842–1910), *Oliver Wendell Holmes Jr.* (1841–1935), and *George Mead* (1863–1931), is regarded as one of the pioneers of pragmatism (Menand, 2002). However, Dewey was unique among such acclaimed philosophers in that he focused on the practical project of school. The American public school emerged in the early to mid-nineteenth century with the moral mission of preparing the country's young population for democratic citizenship. Although the school's purpose is often splintered by the public who seek to use the school for their own ends (Goodlad, 1984), one only needs to look at many of the state constitutions from the nineteenth century to realize the singular socio-civic mission of public schooling. By the turn of the twentieth century, Dewey emerged as a prominent voice that illustrated what education for democratic citizenship should look like.

Democratic education rubs against the natural tendencies of individuals (Parker, 1996). Most, if not all of us, gravitate toward our own inherent selfish and tribal interests when making decisions. We often define heroism as someone who stands up for others. Those individuals stand out to us as exceptional. One only needs to look at who we memorialize and why we do so to prove this point. For those who view democracy as merely a form of government, the role of the public is merely to vote on political candidates or ballot initiatives and referendums. Such a narrow conception of democracy does little to push individuals away from their self-interests. Dewey conceived democracy as much larger than a form of government in that he emphasized its social aspect over the customary political definition.

"Democracy is much broader than a special political form," Dewey asserted in 1937, it is a "way of life, social and individual" (Dewey, 1937, p. 457). This social conception of democracy, which Dewey called "associated living," requires individuals to collaborate for the best interest of the society writ large. Collaboration is central to Dewey's conception of democracy because the best interests of society are met when all expressions of interest are considered. He expanded on this idea in his classic 1916 work, *Democracy and Education*:

> The extension in space of the number of individuals who participate in an interest so that each has to refer his own action to that of others, and to consider the action of others to give point and direction to his own, is equivalent to the breaking down of those barriers of class, race, and national territory which kept me from perceiving the full import of their activity.
>
> (Dewey, 1916/2005, p. 95)

As the individuals in a democratic society consider the best interests of their society, they must be attuned to the possibilities that a group or groups may be oppressed by various political or economic forces. Democracy and individual freedom, according to Dewey, are in unison with one another. A central tenet of democracy, according to Dewey, therefore, is:

> its insistence upon freedom of belief, of inquiry, of discussion, of assembly, of education: upon the method of public intelligence in opposition to even a coercion that claims to be exercised in behalf of the ultimate freedom of all individuals.
>
> (Dewey, 1937/1998, p. 338)

This central tenet of freedom required an educational setting that assured the growth of individuals and, in turn, the society. There is no institution better suited to develop democratic skills and habits than the public school because of its unique positioning in society as a gathering place for the public. The school's initiative, therefore, according to Dewey, should be to position young people to inquire into social problems as a sort of laboratory of democracy where young people can address reality together.

In 1897, Dewey published *My Pedagogic Creed* as a means to share his philosophy of teaching. The central tenet of what Dewey shared was that education exists when students are immersed in exploring and examining their social environment. "I believe," Dewey (1897) proclaimed, "that all education proceeds by the participation of the individual in the social consciousness of the race" (p. 77). An education system devoid of a connection to social problems, according to Dewey, results in individuals depraved of an ability to think creatively toward the solution of those problems. "Mere amassing of information apart from the direct interests of life makes mind wooden," Dewey (1916/2005) emphasized, "elasticity disappears" (p. 228). Unlike the influential education reformer Horace Mann (1848/1957) who, in the mid-nineteenth century, declared that a teacher should address controversy in the class "without comment or remark" since "the schoolroom is neither the tribunal to adjudicate, nor the forum to discuss it" (p. 97), Dewey believed that addressing controversy was essential for the teacher of the twentieth century. This was especially true for teachers of history. "The true starting point of history," Dewey (1916/2005) asserted, "is always some present situation with its problems" (p. 223). Dewey (1916/2005) further elaborated on why the past and the present should be taught as partners in history instruction: "knowledge of the past is the key to understanding the present. History deals with the past, but this past is the history of the present" (p. 223). At the center of Dewey's conception of teaching social problems is the cultivation of a student's ability toward reflective thought. Reflective inquiry, as defined by Dewey (1933/1989), is: "Active, persistent, and careful consideration of any belief or supposed form of knowledge in the light of the grounds that support it and the further conclusions to which it tends" (p. 118). In short, reflective inquiry is a problem-solving approach to education where the teacher creates learning experiences that prompts students to inquire amidst those problems. This inquiry process loosely follows the scientific method of inquiry of forming an inference (hypothesis), collecting evidence (testing the hypothesis), and setting a conclusion or warrant.

Dewey favored reflective inquiry over other principles and methods of education because, as he said, "it emancipates us from merely impulsive and merely routine activity" (Dewey, 1933/1989, p. 125). Unlike reflective inquiry, a disciplinary approach to education may lose contact with the practical and may become too mechanical, thus failing to develop wisdom. Dewey challenged teachers that reflective inquiry, though an approach that potentially yields great benefits, required a cultivation of attitudes among students for it to be effective. These attitudes are open-mindedness (a willingness to change one's predisposed opinions about certain topics, if evidence supports such a change), wholeheartedness (a willingness to work toward solving a problem), and responsibility (a willingness to accept consequences of changing behavior based on the solution of a problem). We will look closer at Dewey's conception of reflective thinking and its necessary characteristics in a later chapter.

Social Studies Today

As we have seen, John Dewey's philosophical fingerprints are all over the origins of social studies education. Yet is this still the case? As you will see in later chapters throughout this book, most innovations of social studies education indeed sprout from the spirit of the 1916 Report to foster educational experiences for students that resonate both with students' immediate interests and with contemporary social significance. Perhaps the most helpful contemporary demonstration of this phenomenon is the National Council for the Social Studies' (NCSS) *National Curriculum Standards for Social Studies*, and its more recent curricular initiative called the *C3 (college, career, and civic life) framework*.

The National Curriculum Standards, first published in 1994 and later revised in 2010, focused around ten themes. Table 1.2 displays these ten themes and provides a sampling of proposed questions intended to help practitioners better understand how to employ the standards in their curriculum.

As you can see in Table 1.2, these themes move away from a strict disciplinary-based approach and instead focuses on themes that sprout from social science disciplines but are crafted in such a way where they may be integrated in any social studies lesson in combination with one another. The questions I provide you in Table 1.2 demonstrate how the standards resonate with inquiry-based teaching and learning. The clear intent is for a student to better understand the world surrounding them, and the themes and questions intend to empower students to do so. In fact, the standards' definition of social studies education explicitly states its mission being intrinsically tied with democratic citizenship. Clearly, these standards are flavored by the social melioristic spirit that also fueled the 1916 Report.

The C3 framework, published in 2013, was created in the wake of the Common Core Movement to better prioritize social studies education in the school curriculum by aligning the field with Common Core Standards. It was written for both states, as they seek to upgrade social studies standards, as well as for practitioners at the local level who desired to strengthen their social studies curriculum. They were not intended to replace the standards. Instead, the desire was for the two to work together in tandem (Herczog, 2013).

The relationship between the two can, admittedly, be confusing. I will not elaborate much on this point other than to say that it appears the C3 framework emerged more out of a political necessity to ensure that social studies education retains prominence in the school curriculum in light of a failure to emphasize it in the Common Core curriculum. Table 1.3 provides a simple layout of the organization of the C3 framework. The C3 framework emphasized a much more disciplinary flavor than the standards. However, there is an emphasis on inquiry and taking informed action as a central dimension of a social studies curriculum. The C3 framework, therefore, is inquiry-based

Table 1.2 National Curriculum Standards for Social Studies (NCSS, 2010)

Definition of Social Studies:
the integrated study of the social sciences and humanities to promote civic competence. Within the school program, social studies provides coordinated, systematic study drawing upon such disciplines as anthropology, economics, geography, history, law, philosophy, political science, psychology, religion, and sociology, as well as appropriate content from the humanities, mathematics, and natural sciences. The primary purpose of social studies is to help young people make informed and reasoned decisions for the public good as citizens of a culturally diverse, democratic society in an interdependent world.[2]

Themed Standards	Sample Question for Exploration: Early Grades	Sample Question for Exploration: Middle Grades	Sample Question for Exploration: High School
Culture	How are groups of people alike and different?	How do beliefs, such as religion or political ideals, influence other aspects of a culture, such as its institutions or art?	What roles do unit among cultures and diversity across cultural groups play in communities, nations, and world regions?
Time, Continuity, and Change	How do we know about the past?	How do we evaluate the usefulness and degree of reliability of a variety of forms of historical evidence?	How do we use knowledge of the past to evaluate the possible consequences of specific courses of action and make more informed decisions?
People, Places, and Environments	Why do people move?	What "push/pull" factors influence the migration of peoples?	How are populations, resources, wealth, and power distributed across regions?
Individual Development and Identity	How am I different from and similar to others?	How do people change physically and emotionally over time, and why?	How do social, cultural, and national norms influence identity?
Individual, Groups, and Institutions	To what groups do I belong?	How do groups and institutions influence individuals and society?	What are the influences of groups and institutions on people and events in historical and contemporary settings?

(Continued)

Table 1.2 (Continued)

Themed Standards	Sample Question for Exploration: Early Grades	Sample Question for Exploration: Middle Grades	Sample Question for Exploration: High School
Power, Authority, and Governance	What is government?	How are governments organized in communities, states, and nations?	What are the norms, principles, purposes, and functions of governments?
Production, Distribution, and Consumption	How are goods made, delivered, and used?	How does the economic problem of scarcity affect the use of resources by people and governments?	What are different types of economic systems and how do they function?
Science, Technology, and Society	What are various types of media, and how do media influence us?	What factors contribute to scientific and technological change?	What is media literacy, and why is it important for a democratic republic?
Global Connections	How are people, places, and environments connected around the globe?	What is globalization, and what are its consequences?	How do location, resources, and cross-cultural diffusion cause tension as well as lead to positive global connections?
Civic Ideals and Practices	What are key democratic ideals and practices?	How are civic ideals translated into practice?	How do citizens balance personal interests, needs, and talents with civic responsibility and working for the common good?

and it does connect the social studies to civic action. Like the 1916 and unlike the standards, it retains adherence to social science disciplines.

Challenges Then and Now

While the mission and practice of social studies education is clearly spelled out in the 1916 Report and recent NCSS initiatives, implementing it in classrooms has been inconsistent at best. While many of the nation's social studies classrooms splendidly reflect the spirit of the 1916 Report, others

Table 1.3 C3 Framework Organization (NCSS, 2013)

Dimension 1: Developing Questions and Planning Inquiries	Dimension 2: Applying Disciplinary Tools and Concepts	Dimension 3: Evaluating Sources and Using Evidence	Dimension 4: Communicating Conclusions and Taking Informed Action
Developing Questions and Planning Inquiries	Civics Economics Geography History	Gathering and Evaluating Sources Developing Claims and Using Evidence	Communicating and Critiquing Conclusions Taking Informed Action

are nowhere close to this spirit. Why? The fate of social studies education in schools runs parallel with the challenges of progressive education in general in the American school experience. I speculate that there are three predominant reasons for the unevenness of the implementation of social studies education. First, conventions hold a firm grasp on how we do school. Reliance on textbooks, passivity among students, and confusing inculcation for education has been in existence since the conception of school in this country. These conventions are more easily passed on from one generation to another in a baton-like fashion than something that requires effort like enacting curriculum differently. Second, a history of education in the United States reveals the persistent presence of a conservative impulse to avoid addressing social problems. We will see this play out in later chapters. This impulse may seek to tame the scope of social studies education toward fostering cultural transmission as opposed to reflective inquiry on social problems. Finally, teachers are not necessarily well equipped or fully committed to a social melioristic curricular approach. The reason for this is associated with the first two reasons but also due to the demands it places on the intellectual skills of the teacher. In sum, social studies education is challenging to teach and nearly impossible for those teachers who are not prepared to do so. This has always been the case. In fact, poorly qualified teachers kept the 1916 Report from becoming fulfilled throughout the country as "the pedagogical demands of the shifting, responsive curriculum recommended by the CSS were too difficult for teachers to implement, most of whom barely met the minimum requirements" (Fallace, 2008, p. 2264). While many of today's social studies teachers are robustly prepared for the field by leaders in the field, far too many are prepared in university programs by historians or other instructors who may have once been a teacher but never have been immersed in the richness of the field of social studies education. One of the primary aims of this book is to help to address this challenge in the preparation of social studies teachers.

Summary

Social studies education was created in the early twentieth century to educate for democratic citizenship. In 1916, the NEA published a report on the social studies in secondary education. The term "social studies" was first referenced in this report, and its creators were staunch advocates of social meliorism. Social studies education, therefore, is a manifestation of American pragmatic thought and closely reflects the educational philosophy of John Dewey. The 1916 Report suggested a series of courses for middle and secondary grades, with only two of those courses being amalgamated courses. All other courses proposed by the 1916 Report retained a commitment to the social science disciplines of history and geography. The focus of the 1916 Report was on how the courses should be taught. It proposed, akin to social meliorism, that the courses emphasize contemporary issues and the personal interests of students. Contemporary curricular initiatives in social studies education, such as the NCSS National Standards or the C3 framework, reflect the principles of the 1916 Report in various ways. One daunting challenge with implementing a melioristic approach to teaching and learning, as the field desires, is the preparation and commitment of teachers in doing so. This was a significant problem in the direct wake of the 1916 Report and continues to be a challenge among some members of the teaching profession.

Reflective Exercises

1. In 1897, Dewey published his teaching philosophy in *My Pedagogic Creed*. Using a series of "I believe" statements, write down your own teaching philosophy. For instance, here's how Dewey (1897) started his: "I believe that all education proceeds by the participation of the individual in the social consciousness of the race" (p. 77).
2. In what ways did John Dewey influence the 1916 Report? Explain.
3. Compare and contrast the National Curriculum Standards for Social Studies with the 1916 Report.
4. Compare and contrast the C3 framework with the 1916 Report.

Notes

1 The NEA Commission on the Reorganization of Secondary Schools (CRSE) was first created in 1911. The final report of the CRSE was the well-known Cardinal Principles Report of 1918.

2 This definition was adopted by the National Council for the Social Studies (NCSS) in 1992. See National Council for the Social Studies, Expectations of Excellence: Curriculum Standards for Social Studies (Washington, D.C.: NCSS, 1994):3.

References

Dewey, J. (1897). My pedagogic creed. *The School Journal, 54*(3), 77–80.

Dewey, J. (1937). Democracy and educational administration. *School and Society*, (45), 457–467.

Dewey, J. (1989). How we think. In J. A. Boydston (Ed.), *The later works of John Dewey, 1925–1953, volume 8: 1933, essays and how we think, revised edition* (pp. 105–352). Southern Illinois University Press. (Original work published 1933)

Dewey, J. (1998). Democracy is radical. In L. Hickman & T. Alexander (Eds.), *The essential Dewey: Volume I: Pragmatism, education, democracy* (pp. 337–339). Indiana University Press. (Original work published 1937)

Dewey, J. (2005). *Democracy and education.* Barnes & Noble Publishing, Inc. (Original work published 1916)

Engle, S. (1994). Introduction. In Nelson, M. R. (1994). *The social studies in secondary education: A reprint of the seminal 1916 report with annotations and commentaries.* ERIC Clearinghouse for Social Studies/Social Science Education.

Fallace, T. (2008). Did the social studies really replace history in American secondary schools? *Teachers College Record, 110*(10), 2245–2270.

Goodlad, J. I. (1984). *A place called school. Prospects for the future.* McGraw-Hill Book Company.

Herczog, M. M. (2013). The links between the C3 framework and the NCSS National Curriculum Standards for Social Studies. *Social Education, 77*(6), 331–333.

Mann, H. (1957). The republic and the school: The education of free men. In L. A. Cremin (Ed.), *The Republic and the school: Horace Mann on the education of free men.* (Original work published 1848). Columbia University.

Menand, L. (2002). *The metaphysical club: A story of ideas in America.* Macmillan.

National Council for the Social Studies (NCSS). (2010). *National Curriculum Standards for Social Studies: A framework for teaching, learning, and assessment.* Author.

National Council for the Social Studies (NCSS). (2013). *The college, career, and civic life (C3 framework for social studies state standards: Guidance for enhancing the rigor of K-12 civics, economics, geography, and history.* Author. www.socialstudies.org/C3.

Nelson, M. R. (1994). *The social studies in secondary education: A reprint of the seminal 1916 report with annotations and commentaries.* ERIC Clearinghouse for Social Studies/Social Science Education.

Parker, W. (Ed.). (1996). *Educating the democratic mind.* Suny Press.

Reese, W. J. (2001). The origins of progressive education. *History of Education Quarterly, 41*(1), 1–24.

Tyack, D. B. (1974). *The one best system: A history of American urban education.* Harvard University Press.

2 Imposition

"Who was Adam Smith?" The students in the classroom sat quietly, almost numb. "Well, he is regarded as the philosophical founder of capitalism." The students remained unimpressed. "Who was Karl Marx?" Finally, Toni Fowler broke the dead silence. "He's that guy who created communism." "That's right. Now, tell me about the differences between capitalism and Marxism." At the spur of the moment, to break the monotonous staring game, Madi ordered the class to get into their cooperative groups and, on a piece of paper, create a T-Chart and proceed to collaboratively contrast the two economic systems.

That night, Madi sat in her living room recliner, bare feet elevated, and proceeded to eat the tuna sandwich she made for dinner. She couldn't help but to think of how boring the day had been. It occurred to her that the next day, she should bring some current events in the class to spark students' interest. Once she swallowed her last bite, Madi closed the leg rest and scurried to retrieve her laptop. She proceeded to pull up some videos and articles on the Internet where politicians make accusations of calling one another "Communists" or pushing forth policies "favoring the rich." She collected a few of these and compiled them together for the next day's lesson.

The next morning, Madi exclaimed: "OK, yesterday, we looked at the differences between capitalism and Marxism. I thought today we should look at how these differences stir up passions in our political life." Fifteen minutes or so had passed since the students first began to read and view the politicians' venomous attacks. Madi stopped the class and began debriefing the series of questions each group had been discussing. "So do you think that Marxism is dangerous or that capitalism enables the wealthy to oppress the poor?" It was then when Ben Scott raised his hand and asked: "Ms. Hobbs, which one do you believe in?"

Madi's heart beat just a bit faster. Her breaths became just a bit shorter. Her lips came apart as the rapidity of her thoughts transformed into spoken words.

DOI:10.4324/9781003372318-2

When the 1916 Report connected social studies education to democratic citizenship, fueled with a social melioristic emphasis on addressing contemporary issues, the field naturally became mired in a conundrum. How should a teacher address those contemporary issues that may not be in line with the values of our democratic society? Should a teacher, for instance, position students to be critical of the dominant social order? What if those positions are considered politically partisan? How politically partisan should a social studies classroom be? These questions are the type that raced in Madi's mind when her students requested she share her view of a politically charged issue. But Madi's conundrum is one faced regularly by most teachers, young and old alike. This chapter addresses this conundrum by first focusing on the moment this issue first came to surface in the field with the rise of George Counts' social reconstructionist philosophy. We then look at more contemporary work on political disclosure in the social studies classroom.

The Rise of George Counts

George Counts (1889–1974) was strongly influenced by his graduate preparation at the University of Chicago where he earned a doctorate of education in 1916. At Chicago, Counts became enamored with the sociological dimension of education and centered his research agenda upon it. After nearly a decade of bouncing between various tertiary positions, Counts found a home in 1927 at New York City's Teachers College in Columbia University. Counts soon became known in academia for his sharp mind and was viewed by his contemporaries as a rising star in the field of education. His work as the director of research for the American Historical Association's (AHA) Commission on the Social Studies, a body of prominent scholars from the social sciences and education who met between 1929 through 1934 to investigate social studies education and provide cohesive recommendations for teachers, earned him distinction among the group's membership (Schul, 2013). The onset of his career at Columbia University and his participation in the AHA Commission materialized simultaneously with his growing concern with the social inequalities in American society. Naturally, as a professor of education, Counts perceived the American public school as the central vehicle to address the economic disarray that the Great Depression had wrought.

Any understanding of George Counts' rise to prominence must begin with the socio-economic climate of the Great Depression of the 1930s. The Depression was an economic and social crisis of large magnitude that resulted in massive unemployment and financial collapse. By 1930, for instance, the unemployed in America was estimated at four million. A mere year later, this number doubled to eight million (Bowers, 1969). From 1929–1932, 15 percent of all American banks failed (Lind, 2012). This economic collapse, to some, signaled the downfall of American capitalism and the beginnings of an inevitable Communist revolution like had occurred in Russia over a decade earlier. There were signs pointing to this turn of events such as "100,000 Americans applied for six thousand job openings in the Soviet Union" (Lind, 2012, p. 270). This led to a group of progressive educators to encourage and persuade American teachers to reach for political power and spearhead the nation toward a socialist revolution. As we saw in the last chapter, the progressive education movement was a multifaceted movement of educators who, in the late nineteenth and early twentieth centuries, sought to transform American democratic society through the American public school. A division arose among the movement regarding the means and methods teachers should transform American society. One faction believed that the educator should identify the prevailing social ills and then deliberately use the schools to correct them, whereas another faction, equally interested in creating a better society, thought social improvement could be achieved through indirect means only. In other words, the former faction advocated for indoctrination in the classroom, whereas the latter faction insisted upon no indoctrination (Bowers, 1969). George Counts stood boldly on the front lines for the group who advocated for indoctrination.

It was the responsibility of educational leaders of each era, Counts believed, to restate their own educational philosophy since "resources, potentialities, conflicts, institutions, and traditions of a particular civilization determined educational purposes, methods, and content" (Gutek, 1970, p. 4). Counts was among those intellectuals who believed that the economic disarray of the 1930s resulted in the rise of an economic aristocracy who used public institutions, like schools, to maintain their power and authority. For instance, he believed curriculum is affected to ensure that ordinary people's lives are not examined nor would issues such as economic prosperity be critiqued. Counts also contended that school boards are usually controlled by a dominant social group that usually supported economic individualism and were subsequently resistant to social change. As a result, Counts urged schools, particularly teachers, to create a new social order. This new social order was a collectivist one where "natural resources and all-important forms of capital will have to be collectively owned" (Counts, 1932a, p. 46). Counts (1932b) emphasized to the progressive education movement that it should "become less frightened than it is today at the bogies of *imposition* and *indoctrination*" (pp. 9–10). In sum, Counts commanded teachers to indoctrinate their students toward supporting a collectivist society. This became known, and still is today, as the educational philosophy of *social reconstructionism*. Social reconstructionism was a movement that engulfed voices of dissent, like Counts', who desired to use the teacher and the classroom to challenge and usurp the capitalist economy in place of a more socialist political and economic structure.

Counts was philosophically braced for the backlash that was soon to come for his stance on indoctrination. Whenever cries against indoctrination came his way from critics, he reciprocated with the claim that all education, in some way, involved imposition and indoctrination. Counts maintained this stance throughout his career, as evidenced by the following public statement he made in the last half decade of his life:

> We must realize that whenever choices are made in the launching of a program values are involved. This is obviously true in shaping of the curriculum, the selection of textbooks, the giving of grades, the organization of social activities, the construction of a school building, the hanging of pictures and paintings on the walls of a schoolroom, and in the selection of a teacher.
>
> (Counts, 1969, p. 188)

The real issue, therefore, was not whether to indoctrinate but rather, "what particular tradition will be imposed" (Counts, 1932a, p. 249). According to Counts, critics against indoctrinating students were adamantly opposed to imposing a particular position in a social cause but less likely to stand up against the inculcation of blind patriotism in schools (Gutek, 1970). Counts conceived education to be strongly connected to the growth of society. In short, Counts believed that the aims of education run parallel to the aims of its society and a democratic society that values justice and equality should be supported by an education system that empowers citizens to challenge injustice and inequality. One of the most influential figures in the development of Counts' philosophy on education was his colleague at Columbia University, John Dewey.

Dewey's Forked-Road Situation

We learned much about John Dewey in the previous chapter. It is an understatement to say his influence on the creation of social studies education was significant. In fact, Dewey was in the center of nearly every crossroads of American public education in the first half of the twentieth century. This included his involvement with social reconstructionism. However, Dewey's involvement was much more nuanced than first meets the eye. In this section, we will explore where Dewey fit in with social reconstructionism but also where he significantly departed from Counts on the matter.

In early 1932, George Counts addressed a meeting of teachers in New York City. This address, like others he gave at the time, focused on the role of indoctrination in the classroom. The caveat of this address was that teachers should transmit a particular political agenda to her or his students to uproot a capitalist power structure that was perceived to have gone awry. The ambitious and renowned professor of education at Columbia University, with dark, wavy hair that sat atop his spectacled face, made a powerful presence in the big city. As he concluded his remarks, it came time for questions and remarks from the audience. Among the group of educators arose an older man. As he spoke, he, too, captivated the crowd. It was Dewey. By this time, Dewey's reputation as a philosopher of education was already well established among the onlookers. According to Counts' account decades later, Dewey said he "had checked the meaning of the word 'indoctrination' in *Webster's* dictionary and discovered that it meant teaching" (Counts, 1969, p. 186). This moment signified a turn, or at least a second-guessing, in Dewey's thinking about the points Counts made as he blazed the trail for social reconstructionism. Dewey's role in this social reconstructionist movement became blurred over time and fodder for contention among historians of education. For instance, James W. Fraser (2001) asserted that Counts and Dewey together "called on teachers to be leaders in building the new society and replacing the corrupt and defeated capitalism of early twentieth-century America" (p. 182). Likewise, Diane Ravitch (2000) characterized Dewey as concerned that American education "was about not only teaching skills and knowledge to children but developing a better society" (p. 203) and that he believed "visionary educators could show the way to a better social order" (p. 209). On the other hand, William Stanley (2005) asserted that while Dewey, like Counts, sought to transform the social order, he was not a social reconstructionist in the vein of Counts since he rejected indoctrination in favor of the use of reflective inquiry as an approach better suited to democratic education. While Dewey did recommend that teachers impose reflective inquiry upon students, he did not see this imposition as a contradiction to democratic life (Stanley, 2005). To better understand Dewey's philosophical dissent from Counts, we should revisit Dewey's conception of democracy and the type of education he believed best supported it.

As we saw in the previous chapter, Dewey's conception of democracy emphasized a social aspect over the customary political definition. "Democracy is much broader than a special political form," Dewey asserted in 1937. It is a "way of life, social and individual" (Dewey, 1937, p. 457). This social conception of democracy, which Dewey called "associated living," requires individuals to collaborate for the best interest of the society writ large. As individuals in a democratic society consider the best interests of their society, they must be attuned to the possibilities that a group or groups may be oppressed by various political or economic forces. Democracy and individual freedom, according to Dewey, are in unison with one another. A central tenet of democracy, therefore, is:

> its insistence upon freedom of belief, of inquiry, of discussion, of assembly, of education: upon the method of public intelligence in opposition to even a coercion that claims to be exercised in behalf of the ultimate freedom of all individuals.
>
> (Dewey, 1937/1998, p. 338)

This central tenet of freedom required an educational setting that assured the growth of individuals and, in turn, all of society. Such growth, according to Dewey, required a commitment by individuals toward reflective thought.

Dewey (1933/1989) defined reflective thought as "active, persistent, and careful consideration of any belief or supposed form of knowledge in the light of the grounds that support it and further conclusions to which it tends" (p. 118). Reflective thinking, according to Dewey (1933/1989), was only necessary for individuals when they encountered some form of problem or difficulty to solve:

> Thinking begins in what may fairly enough be called a *forked-road* situation, a situation that is ambiguous, that presents a dilemma, that proposes alternatives. As long as our activity glides smoothly along from one thing to another, or, as long as we permit our imagination to entertain fancies at pleasure, there is no call for reflection. Difficulty, or obstruction in the way of reaching a belief brings us, however, to a pause. In the suspense of uncertainty, we metaphorically climb a tree; we try to find some standpoint from which we may survey additional facts and, getting a more commanding view of the situation, decide how the facts stand related to one another.
>
> (p. 122)

Interestingly, a significant "forked-road situation" Dewey faced in his professional life was how to address Counts' call for indoctrination in the name of social progress. It was at the forefront of his mind in that New York City meeting in early 1932 and was something he grappled with for some time. The following section focuses upon this grappling that Dewey engaged in with the social reconstructionist movement.

Dewey and Social Reconstructionism

While Dewey espoused a process of reflective inquiry as the best educational approach, his conception of democracy attracted him to the social reconstructionist movement of the 1930s. Dewey's involvement with social reconstructionism became most pronounced when he became a regular contributor to the movement's flagship journal, *The Social Frontier*.

The origins of *The Social Frontier* surfaced from a discussion group of educational scholars at Teachers College in Columbia University. These scholars included William H. Kilpatrick, John L. Childs, Jesse Newlon, Harold Rugg, and, of course, George Counts (Bowers, 1964). The journal project began in late 1933 with the help of funding from a newly created board of directors for the journal, which included prominent individuals such as Dewey and the historian Charles Beard, as well as two small foundations (Bowers, 1964). A wide array of contributors to the journal signified the journal's aim and scope to reach a large audience, as evidenced by the occasional contribution of the renowned Russian radical, Leon Trotsky. Dewey himself was a regular contributor to the journal, even having his own column entitled "John Dewey's Page" that he wrote until March 1937 (Bowers, 1964). The journal was a "hybrid of political radicalism and progressive educational theory" and appealed for educators to "unite with the labor movement" (Bowers, 1964, p. 167). Among the regular topics addressed within the journal was indoctrination and teaching. "Views on indoctrination," the historian Sonia Murrow (2011) espoused, "varied across contributors" (p. 319). This variety reflected a split in the progressive education movement of the 1930s. Some progressives believed that teachers should deliberately address prevailing social ills through indoctrination, whereas others believed social improvement was achieved only through indirect means (Bowers, 1969).

Dewey was a member of the latter group of progressives who spurned indoctrination in favor of freedom of inquiry for students. However, Dewey's break from Counts on this issue took a winding road rather than a direct path. Dewey had great sympathy for the cause of Counts' brand of social reconstructionism. In a private letter to the education activist Agnes Meyer, Dewey shared his concern "of indoctrination of an even worse and more flagrant sort that goes on in schools throughout the country" and that he "can't find it in my heart to blame severely those who want to see some indoctrination on the other side" (Dewey, 1935). The indoctrination that Dewey referred to as being already in place in schools was of the same sort that Counts critiqued: a dominant bias toward economic individualism and a form of patriotism that supported the established economic and political leadership. Dewey admired those teachers who were passionate enough about social issues to lean toward indoctrination in their classroom because, as Dewey said in a letter late in his life to the renowned philosopher of education, Boyd Bode, "indifference under the guide of objectivity is so common among teachers" (Dewey, 1950). This empathy that Dewey had for the indoctrination faction of the social reconstructionist movement led him to his own "fork-in-the-road situation" that he spoke of in 1933 as the beginning point of reflective inquiry. Dewey's own reflective process surely saw that his conceptions of democracy and education should be compatible rather than juxtaposed against one another.

Despite Dewey's sympathy for those educators, like George Counts, who sought to indoctrinate in the name of social progress, Dewey made the choice that indoctrination was not the path that progressive education should venture upon. Nearly a decade after Dewey stood in the crowd that George Counts had just addressed on the issue of indoctrination and shared that he looked the word up in the dictionary and discovered that it meant "teaching," Dewey shared more insight about indoctrination in a private letter to Clayton Miller saying that there "is great ambiguity in the word." Dewey proceeded to explain to Miller about the two extremes of indoctrination. "At one extreme," he said, "indoctrination means the process of teaching – from the Latin *docere* . . . at the other extreme indoctrination is a synonym for inculcation which etymologically is stamping in (with a heel!)" (Dewey, 1941). Dewey (1941) provided his final verdict on the issue later in the same letter:

> So I think that discussion to be fruitful should drop the generality of the word [indoctrination] and discuss rather whether this and that measure or method of education with respect to the meaning and value of democracy should be employed.

Indoctrination, in the form of inculcation, was a method of teaching that Dewey concluded was incompatible with his own brand of democracy that insisted upon "freedom of belief, of inquiry, or discussion, of assembly, of education: upon the method of public intelligence in opposition to even a coercion that claims to be exercised on behalf of the ultimate freedom of all individuals" (Dewey, 1937/1998, p. 338). The coercion that Dewey wrote about was obviously tempting for someone passionate about social progress to cave in to, but Dewey concluded that caving into such a temptation in the name of social progress was, ultimately, counter to the cultivation of a democratic mind.

Table 2.1 displays the similarities and differences between Counts and Dewey on the issue of how a teacher should address social issues. As you can see, both desired a similar outcome of social progress and for students to challenge power structures in society, but the means were vastly different.

As we have seen, Counts' advocacy for teachers to impose a particular belief upon students became well known and is what he is known best for in the history of educational thought in the United States. Dewey, on the other

Table 2.1 Philosophical Similarities and Differences Between George Counts and John Dewey

George Counts	John Dewey
Similarities	
Aspired toward social progress.	
Desired individuals to question societal power and its impact on the population.	
Unique Characteristic	**Unique Characteristic**
Committed to social progress to the extent he encouraged educators to impose beliefs on students that he believed would best address social problems.	Committed to social progress through directly engaging students in reflective inquiry as it related to social problems.

hand, maintained his commitment to reflective inquiry and believed that student action came because of the process of reflective thought as opposed to a positioning of students toward a particular perspective and action step. While these binary views might provide fodder for enjoyable conversation among interested parties, they do not necessarily completely clear up the matter of determining the proper role a teacher should play when addressing controversial issues in the classroom. This serves as the topic of our next section.

Teacher Political Disclosure

In 1986, social studies educator Thomas Kelly published his theory that teachers have options of perspectives before them when choosing how to address controversial issues. Table 2.2 displays these four perspectives along with a short definition of each.

Table 2.2 Four Perspectives on Teacher's Role with Controversial Issues in Classroom According to Kelly (1986)

Exclusive neutrality	Exclusive partiality	Neutral impartiality	Committed impartiality
No discussion of controversial issues in classroom.	Discussion of controversial issues in classroom with an emphasis on inducing students to accept a certain position on the issue.	Discussion of controversial issues in classroom without teacher actively participating.	Discussion of controversial issues in classroom with a teacher's disclosure of their own views in a fashion that models civility.

These perspectives are exclusive neutrality, exclusive partiality, neutral impartiality, and committed impartiality. Exclusive partiality is the perspective espoused by Counts, as it emphasizes open discussion of controversial issues with a teacher playing the role of inducing students to accept a particular position on the issue. This can be a tempting perspective for those teachers who are genuinely concerned with teaching for *social justice*. Social justice is justice focused on inequalities due to racism, classism, sexism, and other forms of marginalization that fosters a disparity in access for resources and positive social standing (Adams et al., 2013). It must be stressed here that social justice is inherently central to social studies education since its primary aim is centered around empowering young people toward decision making for the public good (Misco & Shiveley, 2016). The disagreement discussed in this chapter isn't whether social studies teachers should address social justice but rather how they do so. According to teacher educators LaGarret King and G. Sue Kasun (2013), social justice education entails "the pedagogical practice of guiding students toward critically discussing, examining, and actively exploring the reasons behind social inequalities and how unjust institutional practices maintain and reproduce power and privilege that have a direct impact on students' lives" (p. 1). The operative word "guiding" fits best with Kelly's (1986) advocation for committed partiality, as the perspective teachers should strive to take in their classroom because, he argued, it better promotes students to share their own perspectives in an environment that values open dialogue and tolerance. In this position, Kelly (1986) argued, the teacher does not attempt to persuade students toward accepting a particular opinion and promotes civic development. The other two perspectives did not appeal to Kelly (1986) for assorted reasons. He believed that exclusive neutrality was not possible since it aspires to eliminate most anything about political life from entering the classroom. He also dismissed neutral impartiality as a feasible option because neutrality is not actually humanly possible for teachers, a teacher's silence on political matters may lead to a stifled discussion among students, and students are never taught or modeled how to advocate for one's political position in a civil and tolerant matter in a public setting.

Some contemporary researchers on teacher political disclosure (i.e., Journell, 2011) continue to advocate for teachers to use a committed partiality approach. However, this often runs contrary to the neutral stances that society often expects teachers to take. Political disclosure can be uncomfortable for teachers who fear a backlash from students or parents who may disagree with them. This backlash is an unfortunate outcome of these very students and parents not being provided an opportunity in a public setting to express their views in an environment where other individuals may disagree with them in a tolerant and civil manner. John Dewey might have accepted the committed impartiality approach since it leads students to civic discourse through teacher modeling and provides intellectual space for students to engage in reflective inquiry when confronted with their own forked-road situation.

Summary

The United States was mired in an economic depression during the 1930s. This fueled a rising interest in collectivist economic views that challenged the socio-economic status quo. In education circles, the most brazened force that emerged was the social reconstructionist movement spearheaded by George Counts. Counts boldly claimed that teachers should stop holding themselves back from imposing their beliefs on students but should induce students to accept and act upon a political perspective that challenges the socio-economic power structure in place at the time. John Dewey was attracted to such a passionate approach to use education to address the ills of society. However, Dewey struggled with the notion of a teacher imposing her or his beliefs upon students. While associating himself with components of the social reconstructionist movement, Dewey profoundly detracted from Counts by emphasizing reflective inquiry as the only classroom approach that supports both the democratic aims of society and immerses students in contemporary social problems. Contemporary scholars on teacher disclosure, such as Thomas Kelly and Wayne Journell, advocate for teachers to use an approach they classify as committed impartiality, where a teacher openly shares her or his political view while providing space for students to share their own views in a manner that promotes civility and tolerance. Committed impartiality may serve as an approach that supports Dewey's emphasis on reflective inquiry while still providing teachers latitude to have students boldly address social issues in the classroom.

Reflective Exercises

1. Who do you agree with most: George Counts or John Dewey? Explain.
2. Describe John Dewey's "forked-road situation" when it came to social reconstructionism.
3. Among Kelley's four perspectives on a teacher's role when addressing controversial issues, which perspective do you agree with most? Which do you agree with least? Explain.
4. How can a teacher share her or his political views while also ensuring students have space to share their own views?

References

Adams, M., Blumenfeld, W., Casteñeda, C., Hackman, H., Peters, M., & Zúñiga, X. (2013). *Readings for diversity and social justice* (3rd ed.). Routledge.

Bowers, C. A. (1964). The social frontier journal: A historical sketch. *History of Education Quarterly*, *4*(3), 167–180.

Bowers, C. A. (1969). *The progressive educator and the depression: The radical years*. Random House.

Counts, G. S. (1932a). Theses on freedom, culture, social planning and leadership. *National Education Association Proceedings*, *70*.

Counts, G. S. (1932b) *Dare the schools build a new social order?* John Day Pamphlet.

Counts, G. S. (1969). Should the teacher always be neutral? *The Phi Delta Kappan*, *51*(4), 186–189.

Dewey, J. (1935, April 28). Letter to Agnes Meyer. In L. A. Hickman (Ed.), *The correspondence of John Dewey, 1871–2007: Vol. 2: 1919–1939* (No. 08099). Electronic Edition.

Dewey, J. (1937). Democracy and educational administration. *School and Society*, *45*, 457–467.

Dewey, J. (1941, March 13). Letter to Clayton Miller. In L. A. Hickman (Ed.), *The correspondence of John Dewey, 1871–2007: Vol. 3: 1940–1953* (No. 14369). Electronic Edition.

Dewey, J. (1950, April 1). Letter to Boyd Bode. In L. A. Hickman (Ed.), *The correspondence of John Dewey, 1871–2007: Vol. 3: 1940–1953* (No. 13985). Electronic Edition.

Dewey, J. (1989). How we think: A restatement of the relation of reflective thinking to the educative process. In J. A. Boydston (Ed.), *The later works of John Dewey, 1925–1953, Vol. 8: Essays and how we think* (Rev. ed., pp. 104–352). Southern Illinois University. (Original work published 1933)

Dewey, J. (1998). Democracy is radical. In L. A. Hickman & T. M. Alexander (Eds.), *The essential Dewey: Pragmatism, education, democracy* (Vol. I, pp. 337–339). Indiana University Press. (Original work published 1937)

Fraser, J. W. (2001). *The school in the United States: A documentary history*. McGraw-Hill.

Gutek, G. (1970). *The educational theory of George S. Counts*. Ohio State University Press.

Journell, W. (2011). The disclosure dilemma in action: A qualitative look at the effect of teacher disclosure on classroom instruction. *Journal of Social Studies Research*, *35*(2).

Kelly, T. E. (1986). Discussing controversial issues: Four perspectives on the teacher's role. *Theory and Research in Social Education*, *14*, 113–138.

King, L., & Kasun, G. S. (2013). Food for thought: A framework for social justice in social studies education. *Focus on Middle Schools*, *25*(3), 1–4.

Lind, M. (2012). *Land of promise: An economic history of the United States*. HarperCollins.

Misco, T., & Shiveley, J. (2016). Operationalizing social justice in social studies education. *The Social Studies*, *107*(6), 186–193.

Murrow, S. E. (2011). Depicting teachers' roles in social reconstruction in the Social Froniter, 1934–1943. *Educational Theory, 61*(3), 311–333.

Ravitch, D. (2000). *Left back: A century of battles over school reform.* Simon and Schuster.

Schul, J. E. (2013). Ensuing dog fight: The AHA commission on the social studies' testing controversy. *Journal of Educational Administration and History*, *45*(1), 1–27.

Stanley, W. B. (2005). Social studies and the social order: Transmission or transformation? *Social Education*, *69*(5), 282–286.

3 Propaganda

*"They're taking our money and they're causing crime," Ethan declared in
class. The other students sat in silence, signifying neither agreement nor
disagreement. Madi was left alone to respond. "Where did you get that
information, Ethan?" "That's what my dad said, and I found it on the news
too." "What news? Could you tell me a bit more?"*

*Ethan opened his laptop and, after a few moments, brought up the website
that he classified as his source of news. "See, Ms. Hobbs, here it is." Madi
walked over to Ethan's desk and perused at his laptop over his shoulder. It
was an opinion-based site and was highly questionable. "Have you ever
questioned your news sources? I'm not sure that is an accurate source."
Ethan recoiled: "What is an accurate source?" "That's a good question,
Ethan. I think we should look into that some more. Let's do that tomorrow
at the start of class."*

Change is a natural part of life. However, sometimes change occurs too
fast for people to adjust. The first few decades of the twentieth century
stand out in this regard because of the flurry of technological changes that
swept through the United States. From electric lighting to new forms of
transportation, the technological changes massively transformed how citizens lived. One key area where we will focus in this chapter is the effect of
changes in mass communications upon American political life and how the
field of social studies education responded. We will also look at how that
past response may be helpful to teachers, like Madi, who find their students
engulfed in propaganda that poses as legitimate news to them.

Prior to the 1930s, most people received information from a daily news-
paper. However, the advent of the radio brought both information and entertainment inside people's homes with the simple turn of a radio dial. President
Franklin Roosevelt (1882–1945) understood the power of this medium as
he implemented a series of "fireside chats" to explain his response to the
socio-economic challenges brought upon by the Great Depression. The
wide use of radio also saw entertainment programs such as the *Grand Ole*

DOI:10.4324/9781003372318-3

Opry rise in popularity and, in turn, provide fresh marketing opportunities for businesses and entrepreneurs. It became apparent to many in the country that radio communications could play a powerful role in influencing and shaping public opinion. While President Franklin Roosevelt used radio for political purposes, radio provided a platform for one of the most peculiar phenomena in the history of the United States: the rise of Father *Charles Coughlin* (1891–1979).

A member of the Roman Catholic clergy, Coughlin oddly became a sensation as a radio personality. He hosted a radio program called *The Hour of Power* that garnered a national audience, eventually leading to his formation of a political action group in 1935 called the *National Union for Social Justice* (NUSJ). Like *Adolf Hitler* (1889–1945) in Nazi Germany at the time, Coughlin promoted anti-Semitic views with his attack on "international bankers" and would, on occasion, defend actions of Germany's Nazi regime (Warren, 1996). Coughlin's appeal was widespread as a populist who sought to use the federal government to bolster the value of American currency while also promoting a nationalistic "America First" foreign policy. Coughlin was not someone whom the politically powerful could ignore as the NUSJ had approximately one million paying members by 1936. This popularity can be attributed to Coughlin's mastery of propagandistic rhetoric that swayed public opinion.

Propaganda, as defined by Merriam Webster's dictionary, is the spreading of ideas, information, or rumor for the purpose of helping or injuring an institution, a cause, or a person. It appeals to emotions rather than reason and is widely used in most forms of rhetoric. Concerns arise when propaganda is used by individuals to mislead others or to persuade them toward a particular agenda that may benefit the self-interests of an individual or group. While Coughlin's rise to prominence may be outdated, he blazed the trail for a large conglomerate of propagandists who, in contemporary times, use propaganda to sell or persuade others. We will see later in this chapter how this rise in modern propaganda runs parallel with socio-political divisions in our country. The overarching purpose of this chapter is to examine the curricular counter-response to the rise in propaganda of the Coughlin era that yielded noteworthy pedagogical strategies and tools that may usefully serve the contemporary social studies classroom as we face the current rising tide in propaganda.

The Institute of Propaganda Analysis

Ironically, one of the most important movements in social studies education during the 1930s was spearheaded by the philanthropy of a wealthy and notable businessperson. The irony rests in the fact that such activity ran parallel with the rise of social reconstructionism that, as we saw in Chapter 2, frowned upon the hegemonic influence of the wealthy upon society. Nonetheless, the businessperson was *Edward Filene* (1860–1937) who was known for his ownership of the then-successful *Filene's* department store chain and later as a pioneer in the upstart of credit unions in the United States. Filene became exceedingly concerned about the rise of authoritarianism in Europe during the 1930s and feared its exportation to the United States. He found the rise of propaganda in mass media worrisome in that he believed the American citizenry was unprepared and unsuspecting of coercive messaging then mastered by despots like Hitler to acquire and maintain authority over the masses. In the name of preserving democracy, Filene funneled money toward an effort to thwart the rise of propaganda that he saw as dangerous to the democratic way of life. This became the seed money for the *Institute for Propaganda Analysis* (IPA). The primary mission of the IPA was an educational one: to teach the American citizenry about propaganda and provide them the necessary analytical skills when confronted with the propaganda.

While Filene provide the financial backing for the IPA, *Clyde Miller* (1888–1977) served as the intellectual leader of the organization. Miller was an education professor at Teachers College, Columbia University. He is among the most underrated contributors to the field of social studies education primarily because his most significant contributions were made anonymously under the auspice of the IPA. The most well-known contribution Miller provided the field was his analytical categorization of propaganda entitled "The 7 Types of Propaganda." Many succeeding generations came across this framework in their American Government or civics courses, and it has in more recent times been widely disseminated across the Internet.

In Table 3.1, you can see Miller's seven categories of propaganda: card stacking, testimonial, glittering generalities, flag-waving, plain folks, bandwagon,

Table 3.1 The 7 Types of Propaganda (Miller & Edwards, 1936)

Propaganda Type	Description
Card Stacking	Focuses on the best features and leaves out or lies about problems.
Testimonial	A well-known person endorses the product or service.
Glittering Generalities	Uses words or ideas that evoke an emotional response.
Flag-Waving[1]	Relates a product to someone or something, such as a flag, that we recognize and respect.
Plain Folks	Uses regular people to sell a product or a service.
Bandwagon	Asks people to "join the crowd" and take action because "everyone" is doing it.
Name-Calling	Connects a person, product, or idea to something negative.

and name-calling. Surprisingly, these categories, though developed nearly a century ago, remain useful and relevant to contemporary manifestations of propaganda. This recent wave of propaganda, as you will see in the next section, endangers the democratic experiment that social studies education promises to cultivate.

Motivated Reasoning and Confirmation Bias

We have seen in the last two decades a proliferation of changes with how individuals communicate with one another. The rise of social media platforms such as Facebook®, Twitter®, and Instagram®, allows individuals to connect in ways that were once unimaginable. With such changes in communication comes many positives, such as the sharing of ideas and resources among people. Yet dangers are also abound amidst this new era of social networking. While our collective capacity to collect and share information has rapidly increased in recent times, our capacity to critically reflect and discern truth has not. This is especially troubling because a key characteristic of social networks is that they allow "for the repetition of untruths within self-selected echo chambers" (Journell, 2019, p. 3) and empower political figures and their supporters to rouse up fear and anger so to jolt their own grab for power. This problem is escalated when platforms, such as Facebook®, use algorithms to trace user behavior and proceed to create a virtual pathway for users to be delivered content that matches their own interests. In turn, these users proceed to share this content with like-minded individuals who are busily doing the very same thing. This results in the formation of ideological silos among our citizenry that fosters hyper-partisanship and stifles chances for reflective thought among those caught in such silos. Sadly, democracies across the Western world are currently experiencing decay because of this dangerous development of ideological silos among the citizenries. The culminating effect is that societies where democracy once flourished are now increasingly subjected to an attraction to authoritarianism (Applebaum, 2020).

Thinking about political matters is fueled by emotion as opposed to reason (Garrett, 2019; Haidt, 2012; Lodge & Taber, 2013). One of the key features with the rise of ideological silos is simultaneous expansion of *motivated reasoning* and *confirmation bias*. Motivated reasoning is where individuals seek a rationale or external support to validate their tribal beliefs as opposed to seeking a truthful understanding of an issue at hand (Kunda, 1990; Kahan, 2013). Confirmation bias is where individuals, when faced with a particular matter at hand, "seek out confirmatory evidence and avoid what they suspect might be disconfirming evidence" (Lodge & Taber, 2013, p. 156). Both motivated reasoning and confirmation bias are part of individuals' innate desire to protect their self-identity or standing among a particular affinity group (Cohen, 2003; Kahan, 2013). Rather than succumb to believing in the inevitability of motivated reasoning and confirmation bias, social studies educators must work to cultivate critical analysis and reflective thinking among the citizenry in wake of the rise of the new wave of online communication. If social studies educators fail to collectively act on this prevailing need, we will see the continued rise of civil discord among us and the further fraying of a democratic way of life. Fortunately, as you will see in the following section, the National Council for the Social Studies (NCSS) recognized this problem and set out to construct a solution.

Media Literacy and Civic Education

While the IPA built a solid foundation for civic educators to continue expanding efforts to improve the citizenry's media literacy, most K-12 schools failed to do so. In response to both the impoverishment of media education in our schools as well as the growing need for improved media literacy, NCSS recently made public its concerns through an important position statement on medial literacy that asserted: "social studies educators should provide young people with the awareness and abilities to critically question and create new media and technology – essential skills for active citizenship in our democracy" (NCSS, 2016, p. 183). This position statement also provided a series of key questions that NCSS suggested teachers and students should ask when analyzing forms of media. These questions focus on three areas:

- Audience and Authorship (i.e., Who made this message? Why was this made?)
- Messages and Mearnings (i.e., What ideas, values, information, and/or points of views are overt? Implied? What techniques are used? What is my interpretation of this, and what do I learn about myself from my reaction or interpretation?)
- Representations and Reality (i.e., Is this fact, opinion, or something else? How credible is this, and what makes you think that?)

These questions closely resemble the framework created by the IPA called "Find the Facts" that was amidst a larger analytical tool it called "The ABCs of Propaganda Analysis" (Lee & Lee, 1939). While the categorization of propaganda found in Table 3.1 sought to have individuals identify types of propaganda in use, "Find the Facts" sought to have individuals identify the propagandist, analyze their purpose with using the propaganda, and determine the possible motivation of the propagandist. A key feature of "Find the Facts" was its emphasis on requiring individuals to first pause and reflect prior to making a conclusion. This point is significant because it reveals the IPA had the foresight to acknowledge the emotional appeal that propaganda has on the citizenry long before we knew anything about the pitfalls of motivated reasoning or confirmation bias. What follows is one approach social studies educators may use to combat irrational thinking. This approach combines past work from the IPA with contemporary work conducted by NCSS.

Propaganda Analysis for Modernity

In a recent essay (Schul, 2021), I sought to resynthesize past work from the IPA and fuse it with the question sets provided by NCSS in its statement on media literacy. Table 3.2 represents this fusion that I hope teachers and students alike can use to enhance their ability to analyze propaganda.

Atop of Table 3.2 is a listing of the propaganda types created by the IPA. It is essential that anyone who uses Table 3.2 is also familiar with Table 3.1, as the two parallel each other. It is important that students first identify the type of propaganda they are encountering. Notice that I included the option of "Other" among the list to provide teachers and students some creative room to devise their own propaganda type if they believe they are encountering propaganda that does not necessarily fit at least one of the seven types already provided. However, it must be pointed out that merely identifying propaganda types does not sufficiently address the problems

Table 3.2 Propaganda Analysis Tool (Schul, 2021)

What techniques are used? (Check all that apply.)
____ Card Stacking ____ Testimonial ____ Glittering Generality ____ Transfer/Flag-Waving
____ Plain Folks ____ Bandwagon ____ Name-Calling ____ Other

Audience and Authorship	Messages and Meanings	Representations and Reality
• Who made this message? • Why was this made?	• What ideas, values, information, and/or points of view are overt? Implied? • What is my interpretation of this, and what do I learn about myself from my reaction or interpretation?	• Is this fact, opinion, or something else? • How credible is this, and what makes you think that?

that propaganda poses to the citizenry. This is an issue the IPA faced in the 1930s and unfortunately, I suspect, remains a problem today when social studies teachers position students to analyze propaganda. It is paramount that students practice the process of reflection so that it becomes habitual practice for students when they encounter propaganda. In sum, teaching strategies like the one proposed in Table 3.2 are most effective when placed in a classroom where students are already accustomed to critical analysis. Those in the field of social studies education have known this for quite some time. A well-known study conducted in the late 1930s by Wayland Osborn (1939) concluded that students in the study could not analyze the propaganda despite being able to identify it. The study concluded that true propaganda analysis must exist in a larger curricular effort that promoted critical thinking and problem solving. "It is just possible," Osborn (1939) wrote, "that the way to teach critical thinking is to give pupils long-term practice in it" (p. 16). Also in the 1930s, Bruce Lannes Smith, a political scientist and propaganda specialist in the 1930s, made a compelling argument that propaganda education must position students to critique the motives of the propagandist(s) and that doing so required an education in social stratification. Smith (1941) claimed that "certain social divisions habitually use certain propaganda devices and not others" and that "the reasons for this may be given by the teacher" (p. 256). Therefore, while identifying the type of propaganda is important, it is not sufficient when conducted in isolation from further critiquing the propaganda. This is the very reason why I included a modification of the three inquiry areas suggested in the NCSS position statement on media literacy as a logical next step. These sections are as follows: (1) Audience and Authorship, (2) Messages and Meanings, and (3) Representations and Reality. The first section, Audience and Authorship, focuses on identifying the propagandist and her/his interests. The second section, Messages and Meanings, focuses on identifying the intent of propaganda messaging and how it influences the person receiving it. Finally, the third section, Representations and Reality, focuses on analyzing the credibility of the propaganda message and whether it is based on fact or opinion.

Recent research on media literacy (e.g., Wineburg & McGrew, 2019) concluded that those who are skilled in online evaluations often check the accuracy of a particular website externally as opposed to staying within the site looking for official-looking features that can be easily manipulated such as logos or domain names. With that said, students may need to use other resources to further understand the nature of the content itself while classifying a message as based on fact or opinion. One helpful resource is Snopes (www.snopes.com), which is a website individuals may use to discern the accuracy of material found on the Internet. Miller and the IPA recognized back in the 1930s that teaching individuals to analyze propaganda is a daunting task. The same holds true, especially with how well situated we are within our cyberworld silos. Yet it should be the hope of all social studies teachers that teaching individuals how to identify and analyze propaganda is much more helpful than not doing so at all.

Summary

Democracies are fragile, especially when facing socio-economic challenges. Much of the Western world faced such challenges in the 1930s and, as a result, it witnessed the rise of authoritarianism. Changes in communication, especially the wide use of the radio, boosted this rise of authoritarianism. In the United States, Father Charles Coughlin displayed his authoritarian tendencies on the radio and garnered wide popularity among the American citizenry. This led to the creation of the IPA with the organizational charge of educating the public how to identify and analyze propaganda messaging they face. At the pedagogical helm of the IPA was a teacher educator, Clyde Miller. Miller spearheaded the creation of instructional materials that were widely disseminated to schools and became curricular staples in many social studies classrooms across the country. Contemporary America has experienced a rise in motivated reasoning partly fueled by the wide use of social media platforms where individuals easily receive and share propaganda messaging. The National Council for the Social Studies recently issued an important position statement on media literacy, providing social studies educators a set of critical questions that all individuals should be positioned to habitually ask when confronted with media messaging. In this chapter, I provided a tool where I fused these questions with key materials crafted by the IPA, hoping teachers and students alike will usefully employ them as a means to analyze propaganda and, in turn, counter the rise of both motivated reasoning and confirmation bias among our citizenry.

Reflective Exercises

1. Why is propaganda so effective at persuading the public?
2. What are some examples of propaganda messaging you have experienced? How did you respond to that messaging?
3. What are the similarities and differences between the rise of propaganda in the 1930s and today?
4. How have you noticed or experienced motivated reasoning? This can be within yourself or in your interactions with other people. Provide some examples.

Note

1 Some renditions (i.e., Lee & Lee, 1939) of this propaganda type use the word "transfer" rather than "flag-waving."

References

Applebaum, A. (2020). *Twilight of democracy: The seductive lure of authoritarianism.* Doubleday.

Cohen, G. L. (2003). Party over policy: The dominating impact of group influence on political beliefs. *Journal of Personality and Social Psychology, 85*(5), 808.

Garrett, H. J. (2019). Why does fake news work? On the psychosocial dynamics of learning, belief, and citizenship. In W. Journell (Ed.), *Unpacking fake news: An educator's guide to navigating the media with students* (pp. 15–29). Teachers College Press.

Haidt, J. (2012). *The righteous mind: Why good people are divided by politics and religion.* Vintage.

Journell, W. (Ed.). (2019). *Unpacking fake news: An educator's guide to navigating the media with students.* Teachers College Press.

Kahan, D. M. (2013). Ideology, motivated reasoning, and cognitive reflection: An experimental study. *Judgment and Decision Making, 8,* 407–424.

Kunda, Z. (1990). The case for motivated reasoning. *Psychological Bulletin, 108*(3), 480.

Lee, A. M., & Lee, E. B. (1939). *The fine art of propaganda: A study of father Coughlin's speeches* (The Institute for Propaganda Analysis). Harcourt, Brace and Company.

Lodge, M., & Taber, C. S. (2013). *The rationalizing voter.* Cambridge University Press.

Miller, C., & Edwards, V. (1936). The intelligent teacher's guide through campaign propaganda. *The Clearing House, 11*(2), 69–77.

National Council for the Social Studies (NCSS). (2016). Media literacy. *Social Education, 80,* 183–185.

Osborn, W. W. (1939). An experiment in teaching resistance to propaganda. *The Journal of Experimental Education, 8,* 1–17.

Schul, J. E. (2021). Fending off fake news: Identifying and analyzing propaganda in imagery. *The Social Studies,* 1–10. https://doi.org/10.1080/00377996.2021.19 21680

Smith, B. (1941). Propaganda analysis and the science of democracy. *Public Opinion Quarterly, 5*(2), 250–259.

Warren, D. I. (1996). *Radio priest: Charles Coughlin, the father of hate radio.* Free Press.

Wineburg, S., & McGrew, S. (2019). Lateral reading and the nature of expertise: Reading less and learning more when evaluating digital information. *Teachers College Record, 121*(11), 1–40.

4 History and the Democratic Mind

"Why is there war?" Madi stood at the class, elbow leaning on the class lectern, waiting for students to respond. Madi was gaining confidence as the school year progressed. She had a lesson plan straight from Dr. Ellsworth's social studies methods course ready to go for the class.

"It's when a country hates another country," Nikyah answered. "That's one reason we have war. Thanks, Nikyah," Madi replied. "Today, we're going to figure out why some countries may hate another country and if there are other reasons we have war."

Madi proceeded to divide the class into their cooperative groups. Each group was assigned a war from American history: American Revolution, War of 1812, Civil War, Spanish-American War, World War I, World War II, Vietnam War, and the Iraq War.

"The assignment for each group is to study your assigned war. Find out who was involved in the war and what caused it. Tomorrow, we will use class for each of you to present your findings to the class in a five-minute presentation." Madi proceeded to walk around the class for the remainder of the period, helping each group with their task.

On the next morning, each group presented their war and what caused it. The students were required to take scrupulous notes during the presentations. As Joni Mickelson rolled her wheelchair from the front of the class to her group's seating area after their Vietnam War presentation, one group remained: the Iraq War. At the conclusion of the Iraq War's presentation, Madi asked the class: "What did each of these wars have in common?"

Social unrest and political upheaval dominated the European landscape in the 1930s. The rise of demagogues such as Italy's *Benito Mussolini* (1883–1945) and Germany's Adolf Hitler set the stage for a battle between democracy and authoritarianism. As we saw in Chapter 3, the United States was not immune from this demagoguery. While efforts by the Institute for Propaganda Analysis (IPA) sought to empower teachers and students to identify and analyze propaganda messaging they may encounter in media, the role

DOI:10.4324/9781003372318-4

of reflective inquiry as a centerpiece of social studies education received a philosophical boost from one of its most significant defenders in Alan Griffin. This chapter examines the type of history teaching necessitated by living in a democratic society that Griffin clearly articulated in the 1940s and how that relationship remains central to an effective contemporary social studies classroom like what Madi Hobbs forged with her lesson on war.

Alan Griffin

Alan Griffin (1907–1964) is one of the most significant figures in the history of social studies education. Ironically, Griffin's production as a scholar was not necessarily prolific nor did his outreach extend beyond those who study the history and philosophy of social studies education. Unlike John Dewey, George Counts, or Harold Rugg, whom we will get to know in our next chapter, Griffin remains relatively unknown to the public. Yet if one is to examine the philosophical rationale for social studies education, it is essential to know of Griffin and his contribution to the field.

Griffin was a professor of education at the Ohio State University, where he also received his undergraduate and graduate degrees. He was heavily influenced by *Boyd Bode* (1873–1953), renowned professor of educational philosophy. Bode was among the most well-known progressive educators who, like John Dewey, endorsed reflective inquiry as essential to the cultivation of the democratic mind. It should be no surprise, therefore, that Griffin is most well-known for his clear articulation of this same endorsement. However, Griffin's most significant legacy may be the influence he had on graduate students who later became significant contributors to social studies education, some of whom we will encounter in later chapters: Maurice Hunt, Lawrence Metcalf, Gene Gilliom, Peter Martorella, and James Barth.

While at Ohio State, Griffin was popular among students and colleagues alike (Fernekes, 2007). He was known for having a sharp intellect and promoted critical inquiry in his own classroom. As a graduate student, Griffin wrote two books and radio scripts for a WOSU radio program called "No Corner on Democracy" (Engle, 1982). However, Griffin published very little on social studies education once he completed his doctoral studies. This is especially surprising given the high regard so many in the field give to his 1942 doctoral dissertation: *A Philosophical Approach to the Subject Matter Preparation of Teachers*.

Authoritarianism and Democracy: A Juxtaposition

Central to Griffin's dissertation were the differences between an *authoritarian society* and a *democracy* and the role education plays for each.

Authoritarian societies, according to Griffin (1942), emphasize a "hierarchy of preferred values and habits, a collection of unquestionable beliefs, a set of orthodox attitudes, and a selection of 'things children ought to know'" (p. 80). Authoritarian societies, such as Nazi Germany in the 1930s and 40s, have a specific aim and direction in mind, namely, to support the ideological direction of the state. This results in an effect where the authoritarian society suppresses questioning and doubt, particularly of the values espoused by the state. Authoritarians maintain power whenever the population succumbs to collectively be true believers of the political leadership. This suppression of doubt occurs through any means necessary, including violence, if compliance by the public does not come about with ease. Griffin (1942) eloquently pointed out this feature:

> Steel whips and concentration camps are not the basis of authoritarianism, but only an exceptionally unpleasant consequence of it. The basis is the reliance by leaders, teachers, parents, or other authorities upon ignorance as a guide to the conduct of followers, pupils, or children.
>
> (p. 97)

According to Griffin, the pedagogical features of a child's education are centrally tied to the values of the society where they live. If a classroom discourages doubt and questioning, despite its subject matter explicitly espousing favor for democracy, it would be of enormous benefit to an authoritarian.

Pedagogical practice that supports a democratic society, on the other hand, freely allows doubt and questioning. Griffin (1942) asserted that children should become familiar with a democratic frame of reference long enough to be able to make a choice if that is the path upon which they choose to live. He argued that democratic societies privilege its members to intelligently question their very existence. Such freedom is unheard of in authoritarian societies. Unlike authoritarianism, democracies are less concerned with the ideas and values held by its citizenry as much as they are concerned with the process upon which these ideas and values were formed. Griffin (1942) put it this way: "Democracy is concerned, not with the specific character of the directing values of the culture in which it is imbedded, but rather with the way in which central values come into being and are maintained or modified" (p. 95).

Table 4.1 represents a simplified juxtaposition of authoritarian and democratic societies as spelled out in Griffin's dissertation. It provides a succinct definition of the two types of societies, along with their unique aims, as well as the preferred educational practice that supports those aims. As you can see, democracies encourage questioning to propel society forward, whereas

Table 4.1 Juxtaposition of Authoritarian and Democratic Societies

	Authoritarian Society	*Democratic Society*
Definition	Political power is centralized to a singular individual or small group.	Political power is dispersed throughout the citizenry.
Aim of Society	To support the vision and goal of the authoritarian(s).	To support the citizenry and ensure equal opportunity exists among all people to exert influence.
Educational Practice	To support the authoritarian(s) goals by suppressing doubt and questioning of the society.	To encourage doubt and questioning of the society to improve it for the good of all citizens.

authoritarianism suppresses questioning, particularly when it comes to the goals and actions of the state itself.

While democracies encourage its members to critically examine, Griffin (1942) recognized it was unreasonable for individuals to examine every action because "we need to act far too quickly and far too often for that" (p. 99). Here, Griffin pointed out a similarity of democracy and authoritarianism: the need to trust institutions that support it. As a case in point, individuals need to have trust that their information sources are telling the truth. This may be different in an authoritarian society since criticism of the state is usually forbidden. However, in a democracy, the free press mixes with a free market in such a way that the public has a wide selection of news sources. This is most true in contemporary democracies with the advent of the Internet. With such a wide array of media options available, individuals have a more difficult time gauging what is true as opposed to what is not true. Yet it is not possible for individuals to conduct their own investigative reporting on every single issue of every single day. According to historian Timothy Snyder (2017), individuals in a democracy bear a responsibility to seek out trustworthy news sources and to willfully share those news sources with their fellow citizens:

> If you are verifying information for yourself, you will not send fake news to others. If you choose to follow reporters whom you have reason to trust, you can also transmit what they have learned to others. If you retweet only the work of humans who have followed journalistic protocols, you are less likely to debase your brain interacting with bots and trolls.
>
> (p. 79)

Yet to trust institutions, such as particular elements of the press, individuals must possess the necessary skills to reason and reflect. As was required in the propaganda analysis tool (Table 3.2) in the previous chapter, individuals must be able and willing to pause and critically reflect as opposed to succumbing to tribal-fueled inclinations. If you recall, Table 3.2 asked questions when encountering media messages such as "Who made this message?"; "What is my interpretation of this, and what do I learn about myself from my reaction or interpretation?"; and "Is this fact, opinion, or something else?" Questions such as these require a habitual inculcation among the citizenry. It behooves us to further examine the reflective process and how those like Griffin saw it fitting in education for democratic societies. The following section, therefore, focuses on the reflective process that Griffin recognized as a crucial element to the survival of democratic societies.

Reflective Inquiry

Griffin lauded the work of John Dewey, particularly *How We Think*, as to him, it clearly spelled out *reflective inquiry* as a way of learning that seamlessly fit with the nature of democratic societies (Engle, 1982). Dewey (1933) defined reflective inquiry in the following manner: "*Active, persistent, and careful consideration of any belief or supposed form of knowledge in the light of the grounds that support it and the further conclusions to which it tends.*" Dewey viewed reflective thought on social problems as having stages very similar to the customary application of the scientific

Table 4.2 Comparison of Dewey's Stages of Reflective Thought with the Scientific Method

Dewey's Stages of Reflective Thought	Description	Scientific Method
Inference	Form educated guess as an answer to a particular question.	Hypothesis
Evidence Gathering	Collect data that associated with the topic to gauge accuracy of educated guess.	Experiment and Collect Data
Settled Situation	Arrive to an answer to the question that either supports or detracts from the educated guess. This serves as the answer to the question unless further data is revealed.	Analysis and Conclusion

Source: Dewey (1933)

method upon scientific problems. Table 4.2 serves as a comparison between Dewey's stages of reflective thought, as he explained in *How We Think*, and a typical description of the scientific method.[1] As you can see, the primary difference exists with word choice and Dewey was more succinct by using three stages of reflective thought as opposed to the several stages often used in the scientific method. However, a close comparison between the two demonstrates how similar they really are.

Unfortunately, the scientific method is exclusively housed in the science curriculum for most schools. Therefore, Dewey's stages of reflective thought continue to be perceived by teachers and students alike as a novel approach to both teaching and learning. It is with this point that Griffin's voice is most significant, particularly regarding how history should be taught in schools.

However, prior to looking at Griffin's view of history teaching and learning, it is vitally important to first know the necessary attitudes individuals must possess to effectively engage in reflective inquiry.

In *How We Think*, Dewey (1933) clearly articulated these attitudes. They are provided for you in Table 4.3 with description. These attitudes consist of open-mindedness, wholeheartedness, and responsibility. Without a willingness or ability to be open-minded toward understanding new problems or ideas related to an issue, an individual will not be able to begin the process of reflective inquiry. Without pursuing answers amidst reflective inquiry, the process fails to yield further understanding simply because the individual was not willing to put the work in to investigate the problem. Finally, not responsibly accepting the consequences of discovering knowledge makes reflective inquiry a pointless exercise. For instance, an individual's process of reflective thinking on an issue may lead them to a conclusion that runs contrary to their personal political affiliation's official platform stance on the issue. If this individual maintains their current political affiliation's

Table 4.3 Dewey's Necessary Attitudes for Reflective Inquiry (Dewey, 1933)

Attitude	Description
Open-mindedness	Freedom from prejudice or partisanship so to be willing to consider new problems and entertain new ideas.
Wholeheartedness	Spontaneous and enthusiastic search for answers to a question at hand.
Responsibility	Accept consequences of discovering knowledge.

stance on the issue despite knowing better because of reflective inquiry, then that person is not behaving responsibly.

History and Reflective Inquiry

Alan Griffin was known by his students and colleagues at Ohio State as someone who exhibited great patience with others as they sought to understand issues at hand. "Griffin was more concerned that students learn to think and to enjoy thinking than that they cover material or possess conventional answers to the usual questions" (Engle, 1982, p. 47). This patience exhibited itself most prominently when Griffin approached the teaching and learning of history. At the time, and still today to some extent, the most common approach to teaching history was a ground-covering approach where names, dates, events, and other facts serve as its essential knowledge. Griffin, on the other hand, viewed history similarly to John Dewey in that it served a useful platform for waging intellectual battle with contemporary problems and issues. According to Dewey (1916/2005), the study of history is extremely useful for individuals because of its "human connections" and that it consists of the "activities and sufferings of the social groups with which our own lives are continuous, and through reference to which our own customs and institutions are illuminations" (p. 229). Dewey (1916/2005) was also clear that history should be taught in unison with contemporary issues because "history deals with the past, but this past is the history of the present" (p. 233). Like Dewey, Griffin gravitated to the educational philosophy of social meliorism that was featured in our first chapter. However, the reason Griffin stands out among social meliorists is that he eloquently and forcefully tied the democratic ideal by using the reflective process in history teaching and learning. If you recall from Chapter 1, social meliorists believe that curricular intervention, such as what Griffin proposed in history classrooms, would improve society. What then does the reflective process look like in history classrooms, and how can it be tied to the democratic ideal?

One way of crafting a history curriculum similarly to how Griffin desired is by teaching history conceptually as opposed to strictly through a chronologically based exploration that emphasizes facts. This is what Madi Hobbs chose to do with her lesson on war portrayed at the start of this chapter. While the learning of facts is not necessarily poor practice, they do not in themselves lead students to make connections to contemporary social issues, thus leading to history serving a useless purpose as Griffin conjectured.

Table 4.4 provides three categorizations of subject matter and their definitions, according to social studies educators James Shiveley and Thomas Misco (2009). These categorizations are *facts*, *concepts*, and *generalizations*.

Table 4.4 Definitions of Facts, Concepts, and Generalizations

Fact	Concept	Generalization
"A specific and often isolated piece of information that is believed to be true and which can be confirmed by empirical evidence."	"An idea used to organize a class of objects or experiences, typically one or two words, which may be concrete (dog, chair) or abstract (love, justice)."	"A statement of a relationship between two or more concepts. It is believed to be true and applies to similar situations regardless of time, space, and culture. This statement may be used as a tool for prediction and is often framed as an if-then statement."
Example: Abraham Lincoln was President of the United States during the US Civil War.	Example: civil war insurrection government	Example: Civil wars arise within countries when a large group sustains attempts at insurrection against the government in power.

Source: Shiveley and Misco (2009), p. 74

To teach conceptually means to privilege ideas used to organize objects or experiences such as war, immigration, racism, or totalitarianism. Some subjects in school are more naturally organized conceptually than others. Mathematics, for instance, has addition, subtraction, multiplication, and division. Grammar has pronouns, nouns, verbs, and adverbs. But history is seldom organized conceptually. Instead, history teachers and students immerse themselves with facts such as names of historical figures, dates, or significant events from the past. Facts such as these are believed to be true due to confirmation by evidence. Facts are typically isolated pieces of information. To the contrary, concepts can be transferred from one social experience to another. One instructional approach where historical concepts can be transferred is through the creation of generalizations.

Generalizations are statements that employ two or more concepts and can be used to predict or analyze historical and contemporary scenarios. The example provided in Table 4.4 used the three concepts: civil war, insurrection, and government. After the study of a particular civil war, such as the American Civil War (1861–1865), students can be positioned to analyze how those three concepts apply to that military conflict. The result may be the formation of the following generalization: "Civil wars arise within countries when a large group sustains attempts at insurrection against the government in power." This is a broad statement; thus, it can be easily applied to other civil wars in history to test its usefulness as a statement that can be effectively transferred across the historical landscape. Teachers may then assign students various civil wars in history such as the Roman civil wars (BC 100–AD 400), English Civil War (1642–1651), Russian Civil War (1917–1923), Spanish Civil War (1936–1939), Korean War (1950–53), and the Syrian Civil War (2011–present). Students can then use the generalization they formed in their study of the American Civil War on these other examples to test the generalization. With respect to reflective inquiry (see Table 4.2), the generalization serves as an inference or hypothesis and the analysis of other civil wars serves as evidence gathering or experimentation/data collection. After a time of student research, teachers may then position students to explain their conclusion to their research question: Does the generalization apply to each case? If the answer is affirmative, then a teacher may lead students toward a discussion of contemporary civil conflicts such as the rising unrest in Belarus or even the insurrection at the United States Capitol on January 6, 2021. Such a discussion may center around questions such as: Do you think these civil conflicts will lead to civil war? Is civil war necessary? What does civil war tell us about the countries in which they arise? How does a study of civil war help people today to better understand contemporary civil unrest? Is civil war inevitable when a country experiences significant civil discord? These are the types of exercises that Dewey and Alan Griffin believed would make history useful and supportive in a school's civic mission to cultivate democratic citizens because it fosters students to pause, reflect, and make useful connections between historical knowledge learned and contemporary social problems they are present to help collectively solve.

Summary

In 1942, Alan Griffin completed his doctoral dissertation at the Ohio State University entitled *A Philosophical Approach to the Subject Matter Preparation of Teachers*. This dissertation became a seminal work in social studies education on how history should be used to cultivate thinking among democratic citizens. In this dissertation, Griffin juxtaposed educational practices within a democratic society with those of authoritarian states such as those which were in place at the time in Germany, Italy, and the Soviet Union. At the center of these practices in democratic societies was the encouragement of doubt and questioning, both being suppressed in authoritarian societies as a necessity for their survival. The reason that democratic societies encourage doubt and questioning is that in them, political power is dispersed throughout the citizenry with the goal of improving society for the good of all its citizens. Authoritarian societies, to the contrary, require complete obedience and support of the leader(s) in power for them to maintain power.

Griffin believed that history was a useful subject matter to train democratic minds. He believed that history should be taught in such a way that privileged the type of reflective inquiry promoted by John Dewey. Reflective thinking, according to Dewey, applied the scientific method of inquiry to social problems. It privileged the type of doubt, questioning, and evidence-based thinking that are necessary for the perpetuation of democratic societies. For reflective thinking to be successful, Dewey stressed that all individuals who participate in the practice need to cultivate the attitudes of open-mindedness, wholeheartedness, and responsibility. It was Griffin's vision that history teachers should foster an educational environment that embodied a commitment to those important attitudes.

One approach to history education that resonates with Griffin's and Dewey's emphasis upon reflective inquiry is the formation of generalizations. Teaching to form generalizations require history to be taught conceptually as opposed to a traditional linear format that emphasizes the recitation of isolated facts. Generalizations are statements that include two or more concepts and can be transferred to other historical scenarios. Such practice empowers students to apply the generalizations to contemporary social problems and toward a prediction of future scenarios. The promise of this practice is that it produces an engaged and intelligent citizenry that safeguards democratic life and propels it forward.

Reflective Exercises

1. What are the differences between democratic and authoritarian societies?
2. Why do you think authoritarianism arises in this world?
3. How does reflective inquiry resonate with democracy?
4. Describe your experience with history classes in school. Did it resonate more closely with the aims of democracy or authoritarianism? Explain.

Note

1 Dewey (1933) was more specific in describing the phases of reflective thought: suggestion, intellectualization, hypothesis, reasoning, and testing the hypothesis by action. However, I assert that these five phases are more succinctly represented as inference, evidence gathering, and settled situation. Dewey's five phases are simply an elaboration of what I call his "stages of reflective thought" that are represented in Table 4.2.

References

Dewey, J. (1933). *How we think: A restatement of the relation of reflective thinking to the educative process*. D.C. Heath & Co Publishers.

Dewey, J. (2005). *Democracy and education.* Barnes & Noble Publishing, Inc. (Original work published 1916)

Engle, S. H. (1982). Alan Griffin 1907–1964. *Journal of Thought*, 45–54.

Fernekes, W. R. (2007). Alan F. Griffin, role model for the reflective study of modern problems. In S. Totten & J. Pederson (Eds.), *Addressing social issues in the classroom and beyond: The pedagogical efforts of pioneers in the field* (pp. 135–158). Information Age Publishing.

Griffin, A. F. (1942). *A philosophical approach to the subject-matter preparation of teachers of history* [Unpublished doctoral dissertation]. The Ohio State University.

Shiveley, J., & Misco, T. (2009). Reclaiming generalizations in social studies education. *Social Studies Research & Practice, 4*(2), 73–78.

Snyder, T. (2017). *On tyranny: Twenty lessons from the twentieth century.* Tim Duggan Books.

5   Social Problems and Outrage

It was lunchtime at Middleborough. While the students gobbled down their tacos, a small group of teachers met together in Martha Lange's language arts classroom. Among them were Madi and her colleague in the social studies department, Brent Stanvik. "Have any of you read any of Robert Putnam's work on social capital?" Martha asked the group as she forked the salad on her desk. "Yeah, a little bit," a few of the teachers replied. "Well, I see so much difference between our students now and the student body 20 years ago. I think Putnam was really onto something." "How so?" Madi asked. "Putnam writes about concentrated poverty and how today's children mired in poverty seldom encounter anyone outside of the poverty threshold. A few decades ago, that wasn't the case. Our students once did things together, regardless of social class. They were on sports teams together, they went to church together, and they knew each other. That's not the case anymore." The teachers continued this discussion, with Madi taking down names of books and articles to read.

On the following Monday, Madi welcomed her sophomore section of American history. She greeted the students and laughed with several of them amidst small talk as they paraded into the classroom. She walked to the front of the class, welcomed them again, and announced the agenda for the day and the upcoming week. "As you know, we have been looking at the Gilded Age of the late nineteenth century. Today, we are going to explore how many social scientists view the times in which we live today as another Gilded Age. So I first want us to become familiar with the following phrase: concentrated poverty."

On the evening of November 20, 1939, in Englewood, New Jersey, a short, spectacled professor spoke amidst a gathering of nearly 300 people. This professor's name was Harold Rugg, and the people who gathered did so out of both curiosity and commitment for what they believed to be a righteous cause, namely, what sort of citizenship education should their children experience. This Englewood meeting was significant for several reasons. First, Englewood was located near New York City, just across from the

DOI:10.4324/9781003372318-5

Hudson River. Second, it involved well-known personalities of the period. This provided significant publicity and media coverage and, likely, national interest (Evans, 2007). The controversy in Englewood percolated earlier in the spring of 1939 when Bertie C. Forbes, publisher of *Forbes* magazine, was appointed to the Englewood school board. Forbes sought to purify the school from what he believed were unpatriotic and anti-American curricular materials. Forbes' central target was Harold Rugg and his social studies textbooks. "I plan to insist that this anti-American educator's textbooks be cast out," Forbes (1939) proclaimed in his magazine. However, in this meeting of November 20, Forbes was nowhere to be found, preferring to criticize Rugg from afar in the media. Contrary, Rugg was willing to frontally confront the challenge. In the meeting, Rugg spoke convincingly, both with boldness and logic, as to how his textbooks were unfairly and illegitimately under assault. After speaking for nearly 90 minutes, Rugg provided the gathering an hour for questioning. The chief questioners were from a nearby American Legion post, who, according to reports, received a chorus of boos once they concluded. Most of the people gathered that night walked away believing that Harold Rugg was victorious and so was his vision for a democratic education. But that night bothered Rugg, for he knew the power that authoritarian forces can have on communities. "I learned that night," Rugg (1941) confessed a couple of years later, "the hate and ruthless determination which motivates the tiny minority who would rule our schools" (pp. 28–29).

The lesson that Rugg learned in Englewood on that November night of 1939 strikes at the core of the challenge with addressing social problems in school. Nobody was more adept at addressing social problems in school than Rugg, and perhaps no one received as much scorn for doing so. This chapter focuses upon the social studies curriculum that emanated from Harold Rugg's social studies textbooks in the 1920s and 1930s, eventually culminating toward their decline and demise in the 1940s. Rugg's textbooks possessed the practical purpose of intelligently engaging students in the social problems of contemporary life through historical, sociological, and economic paradigms. The story of Rugg's textbooks reveal much about the challenges that exist with teaching for democratic citizenship. But also, Rugg's texts provide all citizenship educators with a blueprint pattern for future iterations of a comprehensive social studies education. While Rugg's texts were the target of controversy for social conservatives, we must also remember that they were also immensely popular among a large swath of the public.

Rugg's Textbooks

Harold Rugg (1886–1960) was a professor of education in the early twentieth century. His career in some ways mirrored that of John Dewey, as both taught at the University of Chicago and later Teachers College at Columbia University in the same historical era when the progressive education movement was at its zenith. However, unlike Dewey who was known as a philosopher extraordinaire, Rugg was known for his popular textbook series. It was because of these texts that some regard Rugg as the foremost pioneer of social studies education in the United States. His biographer, Ronald Evans (2007), had this to say about Rugg's legacy: "He was the American father of democratic education, and of teaching for social justice, in social studies" (pp. xiv–xv). What was it, then, that was so significant about Rugg? The answer lies in the nature, popularity, and the unfortunate controversy over his social studies textbooks.

Rugg's textbooks were crafted with provocative narratives that creatively wove together history, economics, and geography – all with an emphasis on contemporary issues. Their target audience was junior high social studies students. The books, each approximately 600 pages in length, were accompanied by pamphlets to be used by students akin to worksheets. The first of the books were published in 1929 and rose in popularity throughout the 1930s with a total of 1,317,960 copies sold by 1939 (Winters, 1967). The title of the textbook series was *Man and His Changing Society*. Each book in the series had a unique emphasis as shown by their respective titles: *An Introduction to American Civilization, Changing Civilizations in the Modern World, A History of American Civilization*, and *An Introduction to the Problems of American Culture*.

In the preface of the first book, *An Introduction to American Civilization*, Rugg (1929) firmly asserted the tone of the book by stating he "firmly believes that young Americans can be given appreciation of the significant contemporary problems of living together" (p. iii). This emphasis on social problems surfaced from several essential questions such as: What has the location of the United States to do with its physical comfort? What has the size of the United States to do with its high standard of living? Can the United States, a nation of towns and cities, feed itself? In addition to a mergence between geography and economics, Rugg emphasized labor issues, particularly the role immigrants play in the economic success of the United States. "Every person in the United States today (except the few remaining Indians)," Rugg (1929) asserted, "is either an immigrant or the descendent of an immigrant" (p. 61). Contrary to critical claims that surfaced in the 1930s that portrayed the textbooks as anti-American, Rugg (1929) displayed a sense of exceptionalism and optimism toward the present and future of the United States:

Today we live in a civilization such as the world has never known before, partly because of our location on earth, partly because of the natural wealth of the continent on which we live, and partly because of the settlers who came from Europe. They brought their skill and knowledge with them and were stimulated to hard work and enthusiasm. They came from older and more crowded countries in which it was often difficult to make a living. The vision of a new world, rich in land, big enough for all, free for the taking, added to their courage, their enthusiasm, and their ambition.

(p. 66)

Social studies educator and biographer of Rugg, Ronald W. Evans (2007), provided an analysis of the tone and focus of the textbooks:

My own look at the Rugg textbooks suggests that they were progressive in orientation and relatively moderate in outlook, given the rhetoric of the times. They also contained a great deal of narrative history and dramatic stories well told, as well as stimulating photos and cartoons. They were, decidedly, oriented toward raising serious questions in the minds of students about the social and economic institutions of the nation.

(p. 101)

The legacy of Rugg's textbooks is threefold: 1) they provided an interdisciplinary approach to social studies education that provided tangibility to Dewey's social melioristic vision discussed earlier in Chapter 1; 2) they emphasized present social problems and did so provocatively with a litany of historical and contemporary narratives, statistical charts and tables, vivid imagery, and questions that positioned students toward critical thinking; and finally, 3) they had a social justice bent to them that raised issues of poverty and emphasized positive contributions of ordinary Americans, particularly those who recently immigrated to the United States from Europe and Mexico, as well as non-whites already living in the country such as African Americans and Asian Americans. In many ways, Rugg was a visionary for creating a powerful social studies education that promised to support an intelligent, reflective citizenry who were committed to the country's mission of equality embedded in the Declaration of Independence.

Addressing Social Problems Today

Rugg's vision of an integrated social studies curriculum that emphasized social problems, with particular attention paid to issues of social justice, is a protype for social studies education today. In fact, the flagship organization for the field of social studies education, the National Council for the Social

Studies (2010), defined social studies education today in a way that very much reflects the aims and scope of Rugg's textbooks:

> the integrated study of the social sciences and humanities to promote civic competence. Within the school program, social studies provides coordinated, systematic study drawing upon such disciplines as anthropology, archaeology, economics, geography, history, law, philosophy, political science, psychology, religion, and sociology, as well as appropriate content from the humanities, mathematics, and natural sciences. The primary purpose of social studies is to help young people make informed and reasoned decisions for the public good as citizens of a culturally diverse, democratic society in an interdependent world.

The NCSS curriculum standards, as we saw in the first chapter, reflect this integrated approach to subject matter through its thematic organization. The standards, consequently, consist of ten themes as opposed to separate disciplines. These themes are as follows: 1) culture; 2) time, continuity, and change; 3) people, places, and environments; 4) individual development and identity; 5) individuals, groups, and institutions; 6) power, authority, and governance; 7) production, distribution, and consumption; 8) science, technology, and society; 9) global connections; and 10) civic ideals and practices. Such a thematic approach naturally lends itself toward a curricular emphasis on social problems of today. As a case in point, rather than a strict study of the past in a history course, the NCSS standard of time, continuity, and change puts a curricular emphasis on studying the past in such a way where students may better understand "the causes and consequences of events and developments, and to place these in the context of the institutions, values and beliefs of the periods in which they took place" (NCSS, 2010). This conception of history instruction runs parallel with John Dewey's (1916/2005):

> the past just as past is no longer our affair . . . knowledge of past is the key to understanding the present. History deals with the past, but this past is the history of the present . . . The true starting point of history is always some present situation with its problems.

> (p. 233)

As we saw in an earlier chapter, Dewey understood the gold mine of possibilities for addressing social problems with the context of history teaching and learning. This is especially true if the teacher has a curricular bent toward social meliorism (see Chapter 1). As a case in point, in the book *Reasoning with Democratic Values 2.0*, David Harris, Anne-Lise Halvorsen,

Table 5.1 Reasoning with Democratic Values 2.0 Chapter Titles and Social Problems (Harris et al., 2018)

Chapter Title	Social Problem Addressed
The Blame and Shame of It: Salem Witch Trials	Can the principles of individual freedom and a common culture coexist?
Not One Morsel: The Petition of an Enslaved African Woman	How should our country redress the grievances associated with slavery?
Gerry's Salamander: Governor Elbridge Gerry's 1812 Redistricting of Massachusetts	How should congressional districts be drawn in a democratic manner?
A Woman's Place is the Factory: The Lowell Mill Strikes and Labor Reforms	What is the best means to produce a healthy relationship between laborers and companies?
The Will of the People: Cherokee Removal	How should our country redress the grievances associated with the genocide of Indigenous populations?
A Different Drummer: Henry David Thoreau	How should individuals interact with a law they view as unjust?
Rich Man's War, Poor Man's Fight: Andrew Carnegie and the Civil War Draft	How can our country maintain its democratic principles despite the advantages bestowed upon wealthy individuals?

and Paul Dain (2018) created a valuable contemporary resource for history teachers that positions teachers and students alike to address ethical problems that emanate from past situations but have clear reverberations to contemporary life. Table 5.1 portrays a list of some chapter titles from their first volume alongside social problems that I identified as being addressed by that chapter.

On the left side of Table 5.1, the selected chapter titles from the series' first volume consists of historical events such as the Salem witch trials, the creation of gerrymandering, the Trail of Tears, as well as biographical narratives that involve figures ranging from a slave, a female factory laborer, Henry David Thoreau, and Andrew Carnegie. The corresponding social problems identified on the right side of Table 5.1 are questions that I devised to illustrate how teaching these episodes from the past could help illuminate problems still alive today. Each of these social problems may possess high volatility in contemporary life since they address issues of race, labor, political power, and multiculturalism. These four characteristics, among others, routinely raise the ire of a portion of the electorate. It is the volatility and ire associated with addressing social problems in the classroom that eventually left Rugg on the outskirts of conversations about the social studies curriculum in the mid-twentieth century.

Concern, Criticism, and Outrage

After the 1939 meeting in Englewood, Rugg (1941) proclaimed that "I learned that night, the hate and ruthless determination which motivates the tiny minority who would rule our schools" (pp. 28–29). What was this "hate and ruthless determination" that Rugg referred to, and why did it occur? We saw at the beginning of this chapter that Bertie Forbes attacked Rugg's textbooks as anti-American. Yet a retrospective look at the textbook series determines them to be "moderate in outlook" (Evans, 2007, p. 101). What, then, was the uproar all about?

Harold Rugg experienced a natural consequence of addressing social problems in the American public school. Democracies commonly are seduced by reactionary forces that desire either to nostalgically simplify life to a bygone era or thwart a threat that a conglomerate of the population is compelled to believe is encroaching upon their current way of life. The fact that Rugg addressed labor issues, shed positive light on immigrants, and portrayed the capitalist economy as a nuanced system with both positive and negative components, fueled the fire from certain reactionaries such as Forbes. Rugg was also more outspoken in the 1930s about his disdain for the power capitalism granted to individuals and openly promoted some form of "collectivism" (Evans, 2007). Yet such a perspective did not color Rugg's textbooks. When democracies succumb to totalitarian forces that seek to censor ideas that run contrary to a certain viewpoint, evidence and reason seldom matter to supporters of such forces.

Schools today are threatened by what Rugg saw a century ago as the tiny minority who seek to control curricular practices. Merely addressing certain social problems is enough to put some parts of the electorate over the edge. This electorate is influenced by propaganda (see Chapter 3) that conjures up fear and anxiety that may be completely baseless. For example, the recent uproar over whether *critical race theory* (CRT) has a role in the school curriculum recently led a swath of communities to turn against their teachers, administrators, and school boards out of fear that their children are being fed something dangerous. Critical race theory has been a long-standing theory used in graduate-level education, particularly in law schools and history departments, to analyze the role of race in the development of public policy or events of the past. The recent concerns about CRT initially started with the 2019 publication of the *1619 Project* in the *New York Times*. The *1619 Project* was developed by journalist *Nikole Hannah-Jones* (b. 1976) and other writers as a series of essays intended to weave together an alternative historical narrative that emphasized the significant role that slavery played in the founding of the United States. The writers used CRT as a lens through which they crafted each historical essay, and they aspired that the narrative would find its way for teachers to use in their classrooms as additional commentary to the conventional historical narrative students learn regarding the country's founding. This fueled some political leaders, most notably Florida governor *Ron DeSantis* (b. 1978), to attack the project and, in DeSantis' case, ban it from the classroom for fear that the young Americans would learn only the negative aspects about American history such as slavery and racism in general. However, these attacks were with little warrant since the role of slavery is typically minimized in American history textbooks and few students can even identify slavery as a cause of the Civil War (Shuster, 2018). Some social studies educators (e.g., Drake & Cohen, 2022) have stressed that the project should be openly discussed in American history classrooms in tandem with the legitimate criticisms offered by prominent historians such as Princeton's *Sean Wilentz* (b. 1951) who claimed the project contained numerous errors that led to some false conclusions. Juxtaposing Wilentz's (2021) claims alongside the project's essays, Drake and Cohen (2022) argued, would "enable students to see and engage with the contested nature of historical interpretation" (p. 12). But when there is growing public outrage, such efforts by teachers at cultivating reflective inquiry are threatened by the ever-present urge to censor such efforts.

Harold Rugg was very familiar with this threat of censorship. While a social studies teacher must not allow such reactionary efforts of censorship to affect their professional judgement and practice, he or she should nonetheless be prepared to meet resistance whenever addressing social problems. It is bound to raise the ire of some community members. The next chapter features issues related to a teacher addressing those social issues that a community is most sensitive to opening for exploration.

Summary

Harold Rugg was a teacher educator renowned for his social studies textbook series. The series, entitled *Man and His Changing Society*, creatively put into practice social meliorism in such a way that placed Rugg as a pioneer and "father" of social studies education. The textbook series was widely popular among social studies teachers, as it fused history with other social sciences with a concerted focus on addressing contemporary social problems, particularly economic related ones. However, social studies educators who aspire to live up to Rugg's democratic vision of addressing social problems in the classroom setting should take note of the visceral challenges Rugg faced in the late 1930s and early 1940s by a loud minority of social conservative voices who claimed Rugg's books were anti-American and unpatriotic. While Rugg's textbook series eventually met their doom, the idea of addressing social problems still exists in the social studies curriculum as does a potential backlash against teachers who address them.

Reflective Exercises

1. Identify some social problems in contemporary society.
2. How does Harold Rugg's vision of social studies education compare to the vision cast in the 1916 Report (recall Chapter 1)?
3. Describe a teacher you had who addressed social problems in the classroom. Did it stir any controversy? Explain.
4. Why do you think Bertie Forbes was so concerned about Rugg's textbooks? Why do you think Forbes did not personally confront Rugg in the 1939 public meeting? Does this matter? Explain.

References

Dewey, J. (2005). *Democracy and education.* Barnes & Noble Publishing, Inc. (Original work published 1916)

Drake, J. G., & Cohen, R. (2022). Debating the 1619 project. *Social Education,* *86*(1), 9–15.

Evans, R. W. (2007). *This happened in America: Harold Rugg and the censure of social studies.* IAP.

Forbes, B. C. (1939, August 15). Treacherous teaching. *Forbes,* p. 8.

Harris, D. E., Halvorsen, A. L., & Dain, P. F. (2018). *Ethical issues in American history, volume 1, 1607–1865.* Teachers College Press.

National Council for the Social Studies. (2010). *National Curriculum Standards for Social Studies: A framework for teaching, learning, and assessment.* Author.

Rugg, H. O. (1929). *An introduction to American civilization.* Ginn and Company.

Rugg, H. O. (1941). *That men may understand: An American in the long armistice.* Doubleday, Doran.

Shuster, K. (2018). Teaching hard history: American slavery. *Southern Poverty Law Center.* www.splcenter.org/sites/default/files/tt_hard_history_american_slavery.pdf.

Wilentz, S. (2021). The 1619 project and living in truth. *Opera Historica,* *22*(1), 87–101.

Winters, E. A. (1967). Man and his changing society: The textbooks of Harold Rugg. *History of Education Quarterly,* *7*(4), 493–514.

6 Closed Areas

"Ms. Hobbs, can you please stop by my office during your prep period?"
"Sure," Madi replied.

For the next hour or so, a flurry of thoughts raced in Madi's mind anytime she wasn't active doing something else: Why did the principal want to speak with her? Was she in trouble? What did she do? She was about to find out.

"Hi, Mr. Shatner, you wanted to see me?" Madi inquired as she peeked in the principal's office. "Yes, thanks for stopping by, Ms. Hobbs."

Madi sat down at the circular table in the office, with the principal joining on its other side.

"I got a phone call yesterday from Billie Anne Rinehardt's mother. She's very upset with you."

"Why? What did I do?" Madi said as her heart fluttered.

"She thinks that your class is becoming too political and that Billie Anne is being taught to hate herself."

"How's that?"

"She said that you taught about racism and that you're subjecting Billie Anne to feel inferior because she's white."

"Last week, we finished a unit on the Jim Crow era and, as I always do, I tied that lesson with contemporary challenges we faced today with systemic racism that affects African Americans both economically and socially. I had all the students list famous white Americans and then list famous African Americans. Of course, they struggled to list many African Americans beyond Martin Luther King Jr. or LeBron James. That supported the point I tried to make with them that African Americans have historically been held back and we continue to do so by not featuring African Americans in our popular culture, our school curriculum, and our school community. Every single one of the students who were African American approached me after class and thanked me for teaching that lesson."

"I see. Thanks for explaining. I suspected this was the case. We've got some work to do in our community on this issue. I want to let you know that

DOI:10.4324/9781003372318-6

I'm proud of you and I'm proud to say I hired you. Keep doing what you think is right, Ms. Hobbs."

"Thank you, Mr. Shatner, that means a lot."

Burlington, Wisconsin, is a town of approximately 11,000 people, 89 percent of whom are white. In a nearby town, Kenosha, protests filled the streets after police officers there shot a Black man, *Jacob Blake*. It was August of 2021, and the school year had just started. *Melissa Statz*, a young fourth-grade teacher at Burlington's public school district, decided to address some of her students' questions about the *Black Lives Matter* movement that had recently been receiving attention in the local and national media. These students wanted to know what was happening in their nearby city. Melissa decided that it was important to address the issue in her classroom. She put together a lesson plan that included a children's book, an educational video, and a worksheet focused on the *Black Lives Matter* movement and systemic racism in the United States. Statz, who is white, received a favorable response to the lesson by her students, particularly those who were Black. It was, in her estimation, a successful lesson.

In the evening of the day she taught the lesson, a colleague notified Melissa about a community Facebook® page that was just formed, with 40,000 members, called "Burlington, WI, buy sell & trade." The page was started by a parent who posted a picture of the worksheet Statz used in the lesson earlier that day. The parent labeled the lesson as an attempt to "indoctrinate our kids." The growing membership of this page demanded that Statz be disciplined. She was stunned. The story garnered the national spotlight. In an interview for NBC News, Statz shared why she was so surprised by the public response to her lesson: "People have just decided if you support *Black Lives Matter*, you must be a liberal . . . somehow people have associated those words with a political party. I don't know why. I think it's a human rights issue" (Kingkade, 2020).

There is a pedagogical kinship between Melissa Statz, Harold Rugg, and our own Madi Hobbs. In the previous chapter, we saw how Harold Rugg found himself mired in controversy over his textbook series. We addressed the possibilities and consequences with addressing social issues throughout the chapter. If Rugg chose not to address social problems in his books, he would not have encountered a backlash. In this chapter, we will continue this theme of addressing social issues but doing so by paying particular attention to those issues that social studies educators Maurice Hunt and Lawrence Metcalf called "closed areas." Closed areas, according to Hunt and Metcalf (Hunt & Metcalf, 1968), are areas of interest "not open to reflective inquiry" (p. 293) among individuals and sometimes entire communities. Melissa Statz discovered that race relations was a closed area for thousands of Americans, particularly in the predominantly white town of Burlington, Wisconsin.

Understanding Closed Areas

Maurice Hunt (1915–1979) and *Lawrence Metcalf* (1915–1989) were academic ancestors of Alan Griffin (see Chapter 4). Both learned under Griffin's tutelage at Ohio State University prior to embarking on successful careers of their own as professors of social studies education. Hunt was employed at Fresno State College, whereas Metcalf was at the University of Illinois. In the mid-twentieth century, they collaborated on one of the most important textbooks aimed to prepare social studies teachers. The book was simply entitled *Teaching High School Social Studies: Problems in Reflective Thinking and Understanding* and was published in 1955 with a second edition emerging in 1968. It is the book that christened Hunt and Metcalf among the most significant contributors to the field of social studies education. Chief among Hunt and Metcalf's explications in the book is that of *closed areas*. In this section, we will come to better understand Hunt and Metcalf's definition of a closed area, what causes some issues to be a closed area, and how social studies teachers may best address closed areas in their classroom.

Closed areas, according to Hunt and Metcalf, emerge out of two overlapping forces: interpersonal conflict and intrapersonal conflict. "It has not been understood," Hunt and Metcalf (1968) contended, "that problems of social conflict exist not only as issues between individuals and groups, but also as sources of confusion within individual personalities" (p. 24). An individual who may perceive a social conflict dogmatically may be doing so as a means of protecting their ego and sense of self. Hunt and Metcalf (1968) illuminated upon this phenomenon by stating that "those areas of belief which are most important to individuals are likely to be those in which rational thought is least valued" (p. 26). As a result, certain areas are "closed" to rational thought among some individuals and their respective communities. Table 6.1 displays the problematic areas that Hunt and Metcalf (1968) shared as most closed to rational thought in the United States among individuals and their communities.

These issues include areas related to economics, nationalism, social class, religion, race, and sex. The table explains these areas in further detail along with an explanation of how these areas are often closed to rational thought among individuals. If you recall from Chapter 4, Alan Griffin juxtaposed the differing characteristics of education in an authoritarian society as opposed to a democratic one. In the former, doubt is suppressed and certainty is emphasized. In the latter, doubt and questioning is encouraged. Communities, both small and large, may take on a particular identity based on the closure of a particular issue. As a result, democratic societies often have pockets of authoritarianism that can germinate if not carefully tended

Table 6.1 Problematic Areas of Culture (Hunt & Metcalf, 1968)

Problematic Area	Explanation
Economics	Individuals often view economic policy and the role of government in a dogmatic fashion.
Nationalism, Patriotism, and Foreign Affairs	Individuals often view areas of national pride and international relations in a dogmatic fashion.
Social Class	Individuals often view issues of social stratification in a dogmatic fashion.
Religion and Morality	Individuals often view issues of religion and morality in a dogmatic fashion.
Race and Minority-Group Relations	Individuals, particularly those in positions of cultural power, are often times influenced and feel threatened as a result of racial prejudice.
Sex, Courtship, and Marriage	Individuals often view sexual relations and customs in a dogmatic fashion.

to educationally. Hunt and Metcalf (1968) elaborated upon this authoritarian feature of closed areas:

> Each closed area has a set of sanctioned (albeit often irrational and inconsistent) beliefs that everyone is expected to follow, and which we try to inculcate in the minds of the young through propaganda; no one is taught to rely upon independent thinking for his answers, but on tradition, the church, or political leaders. People who get out of line find themselves in deep trouble; and severe pressure, both social and legal, may be placed on persons who have original ideas in these areas.
>
> (p. 28)

So closed areas often have lives of their own for those who refuse to partake in a rational examination of them. Many times, a culture may exist among individuals who refute rational thought and, in turn, the closure of the area may become an individual's identity – making it particularly troublesome for rational thought to gain any traction among them.

The problematic areas that Hunt and Metcalf brought to our attention over a half decade ago still resonate with us today. In fact, the list from Table 6.1 could easily be mistaken as having been authored in the twenty-first century. One way to illustrate potential closed areas in contemporary life is to examine popular literature that communities either challenge or ban from their respective schools. Each year, the American Library Association (ALA) compiles and publishes a list of books challenged in some communities. See Table 6.2 for the ALA list of challenged books in the year 2020.

Table 6.2 American Library Association's Top Ten Most Challenged Books of 2020

Book Title and Author	Reason for Challenge
George (Alex Gino)	Challenged, banned, and restricted for LGBTQIA+ content, conflicting with a religious viewpoint, and not reflecting "the values of our community."
Stamped Racism, Antiracism, and You (Ibram X. Kendi and Jason Reynolds)	Banned and challenged because of author's public statements and because of claims that the book contains "selective storytelling incidents" and does not encompass racism against all people.
All American Boys (Jason Reynolds and Brenden Kiely)	Banned and challenged for profanity, drug use, and alcoholism and because it was thought to promote anti-police views, contain divisive topics, and be "too much of a sensitive matter right now."
Speak (Lauri Halse Anderson)	Banned, challenged, and restricted because it was thought to contain a political viewpoint and it was claimed to be biased against male students and for the novel's inclusion of rape and profanity.
The Absolutely True Diary of a Part-Time Indian (Sherman Alexie)	Banned and challenged for profanity, sexual references, and allegations of sexual misconduct by the author.
Something Happened in Our Town: A Child's Story About Racial Injustice (Marianne Celano, Marietta Collins, and Ann Hazzard, illustrated by Jennifer Zivoin)	Challenged for "divisive language" and because it was thought to promote anti-police views.
To Kill a Mockingbird (Harper Lee)	Banned and challenged for racial slurs and their negative effect on students, featuring a "white savior" character and its perception of the Black experience.
Of Mice and Men (John Steinbeck)	Banned and challenged for racial slurs and racist stereotypes and their negative effect on students.
The Bluest Eyes (Toni Morrison)	Banned and challenged because it was considered sexually explicit and depicts child sexual abuse.
The Hate U Give (Angie Thomas)	Challenged for profanity, and it was thought to promote an anti-police message.

Source: American Library Association (2021). *Top 10 Most Challenge Books Lists*. www.ala.org

As you can see in Table 6.2, the list resonates with some of the areas Hunt and Metcalf raised as being problematic, most notably "sex, courtship, and marriage" and "race and minority-group relations" were common themes. Interestingly, the ALA reported that some books were challenged as raising divisive issues that were "too much of a sensitive matter right now." This brings us to an essential question for the social studies classroom: How do teachers effectively address closed areas in their classroom?

Addressing Closed Areas in the Classroom

Teachers are likely to meet challenges when addressing closed areas. Our feature on Melissa Statz testifies to this fact. However, these challenges should not deter teachers from doing the right thing by addressing closed areas. Hunt and Metcalf (1968) were very clear about this, and they even tied a teachers' decision as to whether they should address a closed area as a moral crux between democracy and authoritarianism:

> The most troublesome of present issues are over the question of whether we are to become more democratic or more authoritarian in our core values. To become more democratic is to expose closed areas to rational study. To close down further on inquiry in these areas is to move away from our democratic heritage and toward the authoritarianism we delight in denouncing when practiced by foreign powers.
>
> (p. 35)

Whether teachers should address closed areas (and, again, yes, they should) is one matter. How should teachers address closed areas is another matter. Hunt and Metcalf (1968) asserted that "every closed area can be opened up by skillful, tactful, fair, and objective teachers" (p. 27). They focused on two primary areas where teachers should focus their attention to successfully open closed areas: classroom questioning and classroom environment.

Classroom Questioning

There are different kinds of questions. Some questions require a regurgitation of simple knowledge such as names, dates, and other facts. These questions do not promote reflection and are not of the type endorsed by Hunt and Metcalf. They proposed that teachers use more questions that elicit thinking like the cognitive objectives purported by Benjamin Bloom (1956) such as comprehension, application, analysis, synthesis, and evaluation. Table 6.3 displays a representation of *Bloom's taxonomy* of educational objectives as originally designed in the late 1950s.

At the bottom of Bloom's taxonomy, representing a low-level of cognition, is knowledge. Knowledge is the level where students are asked questions that require them to recall information previously provided to

Table 6.3 Bloom's Taxonomy of Educational Objectives (Bloom, 1956)

Level	Description	Question Example
Evaluation	Judge merits or value of knowledge.	Justify Determine
Synthesis	Put parts of knowledge together in a new way to test it and/or create a solution.	Design Develop
Analyze	Separate knowledge into parts.	Compare/Contrast Differentiate
Application	Identify and use relevant knowledge in a new situation.	How does this work in this situation?
Comprehension	Rephrase or translate prior knowledge.	Summarize Interpret
Knowledge	Recall information previously provided.	List Define

them. Beginning with comprehension, the cognitive level of the questioning increases toward application, analyze, synthesis, and evaluation. It is important to note that this taxonomy is not aimed for teachers to use questioning or other educational experiences in a linear fashion (i.e., a teacher must address the knowledge level first, then the comprehension level, etc.). Unfortunately, Bloom's theory has often been misunderstood when put into practice. Rather than the taxonomy serving as a mere organization of the levels of thinking that individuals may engage in, it has been misused as a theory of teaching where "lower order" tasks must be mastered prior to introducing "higher order" tasks (Case, 2013). In fact, some theorists (i.e., Wineburg & Schneider, 2010) argue that the "higher order" skills such as evaluation should be stressed much earlier than what proponents of Bloom's taxonomy espouse. Again, it is important to note that the taxonomy is not a theory of teaching. It may very well be the case that individuals who are engaged in thinking at the comprehension level – for instance – will jump immediately to the evaluation level of thinking and vice versa. However, Hunt and Metcalf did emphasize that questioning which elicited the type of thinking that would best open closed areas in the classroom would be those above the knowledge level. Figure 6.1 displays the samples of questions that Hunt and Metcalf (1968) provided to illustrate their stance.

As you will notice, these questions require individuals to reflect prior to answering. Many of these questions require the student to make a decision by asking them "how" or "why" or "which" followed by a directive. Hunt and Metcalf should not be looked upon as possessing the perfect approach

"Why do you say that?"
"Do you agree or disagree and why?"
"If you believe such-and-such, then how can you believe so-and-so?"
"Is such-and-such behavior [or belief] consistent with so-and-so behavior or belief?"
"What would you do in a case like this?"
"How do you explain this fact?"
"Why do you believe that?"
"Why do you think that so many people in our community believe so-and-so?"
"If you did that, what might the results be?"
"Can you define that clearly, and give us some examples?"
"What does this statement mean?"
"What other way could you say it?"
"Can you give an example or illustration of this?"
"How would you define this word?"
"How could we prove or disprove a statement like this?"
"How can we get facts which will answer this?"
"How reliable are such data?"
"What do these facts mean?"
"What can we conclude from a study of these data?"
"Which consequences do you prefer?"

Figure 6.1 Sample Questions from Hunt and Metcalf (1968, p. 181)

to using Bloom's taxonomy, but they did use it to help teachers better understand how to elicit certain type of thinking from students by employing certain types of questioning. An example of an interaction between students and a teacher might go in this manner:

Teacher: Lately, several professional athletes are choosing to kneel at the playing of the national anthem in protest of what they see as discrimination by police against African Americans. Do you agree or disagree with what they're doing and why?
Student: I don't think we should ever disrespect the flag, especially those who served in the Armed Forces who fought to defend that flag. It is unpatriotic of them to do this.
Teacher: What other way would you prefer that they protest?
Student: Well, the flag is off-limits. Maybe they should write a letter to the President.
Teacher: Would we be talking about this issue if they wrote a letter to the President?
Student: I just think that if you don't like the freedom we have in this country, then you should just leave it for somewhere else.
Teacher: If you value freedom, then why do you want to stop these athletes from exercising their freedom?

Of course, most teachers realize that such exchanges they have with students can go in a myriad of directions. However, the point here is for the teacher to continue with a line of questioning that provokes the student to reflectively think. It is especially important to recognize that the student very well may continue to speak in defense of their original perspective. It is in human nature to defend oneself. However, this does not mean that the questioning by the teacher was a futile exercise. The teacher should be patient with her or his students since cultivating reflective thinking is a delicate matter that requires the teacher to foster a caring classroom environment. This leads to Hunt and Metcalf's other factor necessary for teachers to successfully open closed areas: the classroom environment.

Classroom Environment

The fruitfulness of questioning as a means of evoking reflective thought among students hinges upon how safe students feel in their classroom. If the classroom environment is one where students may freely express or choose to not express their views, students are much more likely to be open to new ideas or accept any challenges to their current beliefs. This is the stance that Hunt and Metcalf took in their guidance for how teachers may effectively address closed areas in the classroom. "It is essential," Hunt and Metcalf (1968) asserted, "that a teacher manage discussion so that students feel relaxed, in a good mood, and free from threat" (p. 211). Yet how may teachers create such a classroom environment and what might that environment look like?

One feature that Hunt and Metcalf emphasized in fostering an environment conducive to opening closed areas is permissiveness. In other words, students should feel free to share their opinions with the entire class. According to Hunt and Metcalf, a prerequisite for such permissiveness is one where the teacher refrains from sharing their own perspective. The next section is an example of a dialogue between a student (Charles) and his teacher about a presidential election that Hunt and Metcalf (1968) used to illustrate what such a permissive classroom environment might look like.

Charles: On this election I'm caught right in the middle. Dad's for the Democratic candidate and mother's for the Republican.
Teacher: And whom are you supporting?
Charles: I just can't decide – I think a person ought to vote for the man, not the party. Which do you think is the better man?
Teacher: Even if I wanted to try to help you decide, I couldn't until you told us what you mean by "better" – what is it you want in a President?

Charles: Well, that's not easy. You make a problem out of it. I suppose honest might be one thing.

Teacher: Okay. Why don't you make a list of the qualities you think the candidate should have and then try to see which man fits best?

Charles: If I make a list, then will you give me your opinion as to which candidate I ought to support?

Teacher: I'm afraid not. You will have to decide. But I can help you find what biographical material there is on each candidate.

(p. 213).

As you can see, the teacher sought to propel Charles to think more reflectively by asking him how he defined "better" when identifying a better candidate. Hunt and Metcalf also positioned the teacher to be politically neutral, something very different than what George Counts and his conceptualization of social reconstructionism touted. To Hunt and Metcalf, the neutrality of the teacher was central to evoking reflective thought among the students since it may be the case that students would think and speak more freely if they did not feel as if their teacher took sides with or against them. However, some contemporary research in social studies education (i.e., Journell, 2016) reveals that there are benefits associated with teachers disclosing their political views with their students.

Social studies teachers generally hold fast to the belief espoused by Hunt and Metcalf that they should be neutral when in the act of teaching (Journell, 2016). One significant critique of this view is that the very nature of teaching is a political act and the guise of neutrality can be a way of indoctrinating students. For instance, a teacher's choice to remain neutral may be a decision she or he makes that supports the status quo (Callan, 2011; Jensen, 2007; Journell, 2016; Reich, 2007). Social studies educator Wayne Journell (2016) claimed that even teachers who strive to be politically neutral in the classroom often do discreet things such as making references that are either favorable or unfavorable about a particularly political party or politician. As a result of such discreet practices common among teachers, politically astute students usually can uncover their teachers' political leanings, whereas those who are not politically astute take the teacher's comments as fact "due to the natural authority given to teachers as content experts" (Journell, 2016, p. 103). It is important to note that research (e.g., Journell, 2011; Niemi & Junn, 1998) suggests that most high school students are not politically astute. This means that teachers who strive toward neutrality may do the very thing that they sought to avoid, namely, indoctrinate students as opposed to promote reflective inquiry.

One approach teachers may use when addressing closed areas in the classroom that promises to yield a classroom environment conducive to reflective thought is what social studies researcher Thomas Kelly (1986) called *committed impartiality*. You may recall from Chapter 2 that Kelly outlined four stances teachers may take when addressing controversial issues: exclusive neutrality (avoiding controversial issues altogether), exclusive partiality (seek to convince students of a particular view), neutral impartiality (address controversial issues but teacher does not express their own view), and finally committed impartiality (see Table 2.2). Committed impartiality, according to Kelly, is a position a teacher takes that is loyal to a particular perspective but also impartial in the sense that she or he strives to not sway student opinion by modeling a thinking process of defending a stance as opposed to advocating for a particular outcome of the students' thinking. However, committed impartiality is not the stance proposed by Hunt and Metcalf who preferred what Kelly called *neutral impartiality*. This stance where a teacher addresses controversial issues but declines to disclose their own perspective on a particular issue is commonly and comfortably practiced by social studies teachers. But, as Journell (2016) pointed out, neutrality is an impossible goal for teachers to reach and, in the process of doing so, may harm chances for cultivating students' reflective thought.

The disposition of the teacher is closely tied to the stance they take on controversial issues and whether they are successful with opening closed areas in their classroom. Hunt and Metcalf were well ahead of their time when they emphasized this point. Contemporary research from social psychologist Jonathan Haidt (2012) confirms that rationality is significantly influenced, if not primarily led, by an impulsive emotional system. In turn, individuals are more likely to be open to new or conflicting ideas if they were presented in an environment where the individuals' emotional system is taken into consideration. For instance, a student who is presented a topic such as "Should flag burning be permissible in the United States?" may more likely consider viewpoints from their classmates or the teacher if their own viewpoint was taken seriously in the conversation. In this process, it is crucial for teachers to recognize that a student's current articulation of a viewpoint may not be their final conclusion of the issue if that student is equipped with the necessary skills and dispositions necessary for reflective inquiry to take place. With that said, Melissa Statz may have done everything right according to Hunt and Metcalf in opening the closed area of race and racism in her classroom and she still experienced hostility. Now, the question is whether that hostility came from her students or the community at large. All signs point that it was the latter. A social studies teacher who opens closed areas in the classroom can only reasonably prepare their classroom environment for reflective inquiry. Those on the outside of the classroom who seek to restrict a social studies teacher's opening of closed areas are outside of the teacher's realm of influence. It can only be hoped that such scrutiny is equally met with opposition that supports the teacher's professional judgement and curricular practice.

Summary

To successfully mature, democracies need a culture where their citizenry can openly discuss and deliberate any topic at hand. Whether or not the citizenry is able to do that is a signal of the health of the democracy. One of the jobs of a social studies teacher is to assist young citizens in doing the very thing of confronting issues that they may feel uncomfortable with or, at the time, even unable to confront. Such issues are what Maurice Hunt and Lawrence Metcalf called "closed areas." To open closed areas requires skill both in the form of questioning and cultivating a classroom environment conducive to reflective thought. When addressing closed areas, such as race and racism, successful social studies teachers equip students with higher-order thinking skills and a sturdy interpersonal skill set. It should be expected that teachers will be criticized for opening closed areas. It should also be expected of the citizenry who supports the cultivation of the democratic mind that such criticism is outmatched by a growing advocacy on their part. Albeit uncomfortable at times, teachers who successfully open closed areas are strengthening the citizenry by limiting the likelihood it will succumb to tribalism on social issues, improves its problem solving, and, in turn, strengthen public policy.

Reflective Exercises

1. Table 6.1 displays Hunt and Metcalf's listing of problematic areas in culture that are likely "closed" in some communities. This list was formed in 1968. Is it still pertinent to contemporary times? Are there any areas you think are no longer problematic today? Are there are any areas from today that you would add to the list? Explain.
2. Have you ever experienced censorship of literature or curriculum? If so, what was it? Why and how was it censored? If not, what are some aspects of society today that you have heard are susceptible to censorship? Why and how are those aspects censored?
3. Describe a situation where one of your teachers successfully opened a closed area in a classroom. Describe a situation where a teacher was not so successful in doing so.
4. How is addressing closed areas connected to democratic life?

References

Bloom, B. S. (1956). *Taxonomy of educational objectives, cognitive domain*. Longmans, Green.

Callan, E. (2011). When to shut students up: Civility, silencing, and free speech. *Theory and Research in Education, 9*, 3–22.

Case, R. (2013). The unfortunate consequences of Bloom's taxonomy. *Social Education, 77*(4), 196–200.

Haidt, J. (2012). *The righteous mind: Why good people are divided by politics and religion.* Vintage.

Hunt, M. P., & Metcalf, L. E. (1968). *Teaching high school social studies: Problems in reflective thinking and social understanding.* Harper & Row.

Jensen, R. (2007). Patriotism is a bad idea at a dangerous time. In J. Westheimer (Ed.), *Pledging allegiance: The politics of patriotism in America's schools* (pp. 75–86). Teachers College Press.

Journell, W. (2011). The disclosure dilemma in action: A qualitative look at the effect of teacher disclosure on classroom instruction. *Journal of Social Studies Research, 35,* 217–244.

Journell, W. (2016). Making a case for teacher political disclosure. *Journal of Curriculum Theorizing, 31*(1).

Kelly, T. E. (1986). Discussing controversial issues: Four perspectives on the teacher's role. *Theory and Research in Social Education, 14,* 113–138.

Kingkade, T. (2020, October 24). How one teacher's Black Lives Matter lesson divided a small *Wisconsin town. NBC News.* www.nbcnews.com/news/us-news/how-one-teacher-s-black-lives-matter-lesson-divided-small-n1244566.

Niemi, R. G., & Junn, J. (1998). *Civic education: What makes students learn.* Yale University Press.

Reich, W. (2007). Deliberative democracy in the classroom: A sociological view. *Journal of Educational Theory, 57,* 187–197.

Wineburg, S., & Schneider, J. (2010). Was Bloom's Taxonomy pointed in the wrong direction? *Phi Delta Kappan, 91*(4), 56–61.

7   Disciplinary Thinking

"OK, everybody, get out your laptops." The class members collectively rummaged through their backpacks as they heeded Madi's orders.

"On your course page, you will find that I gave you several documents for today. I want you to spend some time individually looking over these documents. After doing so, I want you to answer the following question in your history journal: What was World War II like for American citizens?"

On the webpage, the students found various letters. One was from an American soldier to his wife. One was from a Japanese American describing his experiences in an internment camp. Another was from a woman working in a factory, as she wrote to some friends from her hometown. Yet another was from an older man writing to a friend about the war.

"Ms. Hobbs," Lin Yang asked, "how can I know what the war was like for American citizens when each of these people had a different experience?"

"That's the point, Lin. I want you to know about those various experiences. Just like today, people experience events based on their own circumstances. I want you to understand that."

A new political and scientific era began on October 4, 1957, with the Soviet Union's launching of *Sputnik*, the world's first artificial satellite. This had significant ramifications for American educational policy and practice. The overarching belief in the United States in the wake of Sputnik was that the country needed to take an aggressive, collective effort to transform its educational system to better prepare its citizenry for the intellectual demands necessitated by this new scientific era. This fervor paved the way for government action. The United States government was aggressive with pursuing this educational aim by passing the National Defense Education Act (NDEA) in 1958 with the intent to "upgrade schools with the growing postwar Soviet threat" leading to "an intense and extensive reassessment of the entire American educational system" (Byford & Russell, 2007, p. 41). The result was massive federal funding of curriculum projects.

DOI:10.4324/9781003372318-7

Among these federally funded curriculum projects were nearly 50 related to the teaching of the social sciences. These projects sought to instill academic rigor in the secondary school experience, and it was believed at the time by the leaders of the projects that such academic rigor came with an emphasis on the academic disciplines. In the social studies, this meant that the goal of social studies was to empower students to become junior historians and social scientists (Evans, 2010). This new trajectory in social studies education toward the academic disciplines became known as *"the new social studies"* and had a significant effect on the field of social studies education that remains today. The intellectual basis of this emphasis on the disciplines came partly from the psychologist *Jerome Bruner* (1915–2016) whose 1960 book, *The Process of Education*, claimed that history was more than a description of the past but a process in and of itself that paved the way for that description. "Knowing how something is put together," Bruner (1960) asserted, "allows you to go beyond it" (p. 183). In other words, intellectual development for an individual occurs when they are immersed in disciplinary thinking. The curriculum project leaders thought this to be the case not only for history but other social sciences as well.

While the new social studies emerged out of a perceived national security threat during the Cold War with the Soviet launching of Sputnik, the initiative also came along at a time when a triad of historical episodes sought for a change in social studies education. According to historian Ronald Evans (2010), the first episode (1939–1942) was the controversy surrounding Harold Rugg's textbooks that we saw in an earlier chapter. The second episode (1942–1944) was the controversy surrounding the teaching of American history that emanated from a *New York Times Magazine* article written by noted historian *Allan Nevins* who charged that students were no longer adequately learning American history in school. The third episode (1947–1959) was the controversy over progressive education by education critics such as *Arthur Bestor* (1953) who charged that much of what happened in schools was anti-intellectual and served as a communist threat to American society. The landscape of American public education was, therefore, ripe for something fresh that promised to satisfy the conservative push for increased academic rigor that moved away from a melioristic focus on social progress (Evans, 2010).

This chapter delves into the work of one prominent figure of the new social studies movement, Edwin Fenton, who some regard to be the leader of the movement (Cude, 2010). This work, I will argue in the chapter, rhymes closely with the signature pedagogy and inquiry-based learning in the contemporary literature and practices of social studies education. This rhythmic pattern will be closely pointed out through an analysis of some contemporary trends in social studies education. But, first, let us have a look at Edwin Fenton and his attempt to revolutionize the social studies classroom.

Edwin Fenton

Of all the contributors to the field of social studies education that we've looked at thus far, *Edwin Fenton* (1921–2020) had the most unique background. In an educational field, Fenton was a professor of history as opposed to education. Fenton (1967) admitted that his background was quirky in relation to the work he chose to take on:

> I am a historian, not a sociologist, a political scientist or a member of a department of education. I have taught secondary school students, undergraduates, and graduates for sixteen years, but I have never taught in elementary school. I have worked primarily with able students, not with the disadvantaged or even the average. I have been closely associated with programs of teacher preparation at both the undergraduate levels at Carnegie Institute of Technology, not at a college which devotes most of its resources to the education of teachers.
>
> (p. vii)

Yet Fenton is known exclusively as a pedagogue who sought to revolutionize the way teachers teach and students learn social studies. The very idea of inquiry-based learning, now central to history education, is often attributed to him (Cude, 2010). Fenton was a curious and creative intellectual whose entrepreneurial spirit paved the way for him to divert from a conventional scholarly track in the field of history and move toward improving the situation for how teachers and students alike approach learning social studies.

When the new social studies movement blossomed, Fenton was a young history professor at Carnegie Mellon University in Pittsburgh, Pennsylvania. Prior to earning a doctorate in history from Harvard, Fenton spent four years (1950–1954) teaching history in Boston at an all-girls high school. His experience with the antiquated curriculum at this high school fueled his passion for improving pedagogical practices in history (Cude, 2010). His primary contribution to the new social studies movement was his small yet impactful 1967 book, *The New Social Studies*, as well as his role as the general editor and director of the curriculum center for the Carnegie Mellon Social Studies Curriculum that included seven courses for high school students. Yet it was his book *The New Social Studies* that caused both Fenton and the new social studies movement to be central to changes made to history teaching and learning in the 1960s and 1970s.

Toward Inquiry-Based Learning

Unlike the emphasis on democratic citizenship that was so prominent in Alan Griffin's conception of social studies education, Fenton saw social studies education as serving a more complex threefold purpose in American society. "Social studies prepare children to be good citizens," Fenton (1967) declared, but he also emphasized, "social studies teach children how to think" and "social studies pass on the cultural heritage" (p. 1). In other words, Fenton saw distinctions in these three popular conceptions of social studies education. Thinking and historical knowledge served individual and cultural purposes apart from the perpetuation of cultivating democratic citizenship. This is different from Griffin who saw democratic citizenship as an all-encompassing aim of social studies education for which reflective thought and historical knowledge served. If you recall from earlier chapters, social meliorism was at the heart of the social studies education espoused by Dewey, Griffin, and Rugg. They believed that historical knowledge was useful in solving social problems. Fenton, on the other hand, saw historical knowledge serving a purpose outside of its ability to address contemporary social problems. However, Fenton was no opponent of reflective inquiry. To the contrary, Fenton hailed John Dewey's (1933) statement on reflective inquiry in *How We Think* and believed that the new social studies projects "would delight Mr. Dewey and his followers" and that "Dewey could easily have sired the majority of teaching strategies developed by the current social studies projects" (Fenton, 1967, pp. 31–32). So what was it that Fenton saw in the new social studies projects that he believed was so staunchly Deweyan? The answer lies in their emphasis upon inquiry.

Unlike critics of progressive education in the mid-twentieth century who believed that students weren't receiving a strong history education because of a lack of exposure to subject matter, Fenton believed that the primary culprit of poor education was direct (expository) instruction. Like Hunt and Metcalf, Fenton believed that questions help to propel students' thinking.

However, Fenton did not believe that questioning by the teacher should be viewed as a final stage of effective teaching practice. Rather, Fenton sought a classroom climate where students learned autonomously much akin to what Bruner (1960) emphasized as a process of education. Figure 7.1 displays Fenton's continuum of teaching that he believed spelled out the three primary practices of teachers and the educational format that each practice fostered. On the far left of the continuum was exposition where the teacher provided information (or cues, as Fenton called it) that revealed information

Exposition	*Directed Discussion*	*Discovery*
(all cues)	*(questions as cues)*	*(no cues)*

Figure 7.1 Edwin Fenton's Teaching Continuum (Fenton, 1967, p. 33)

to the students. The middle part of the continuum was discussion directed by the teacher using questioning as cues to learning. The far-right part of the continuum, however, was where students were provided no cues to learning. This far-right practice displayed in the continuum was called "discovery" and Fenton believed it ideal because students were learning autonomously. He tied this type of learning to Dewey's stages of reflective thought that we saw in an earlier chapter (i.e., inference, evidence gathering, and the formation of a settled situation) that resonated well with the scientific method. It was this autonomous learning that led Fenton (1967) to believe the new social studies was a curriculum revolution for teaching and learning in schools. Indeed, many students found the new social studies projects to be revolutionary in how they learned. Take, for example, what teacher educator and historian Barbara Slater Stern (2010) said upon reflection about her first encounter with these projects:

> When I was in the sixth grade, our teacher told us that we were going to try something new and we would be rotating classrooms for part of the day. We would have science with him, social studies with another teacher and mathematics with a third teacher. In the science class new materials appeared: microscopes, Petri dishes, slides, and so forth. In social studies we learned geography and prepared reports on what we now term "developing" nations. Students became involved in class instruction in a different way than we had for the first half of the year and it was exciting.
>
> (p. xiii)

Stern's excitement in her second half of sixth grade was because "students became involved in class instruction." Fenton classified this type of involvement as "discovery," and he believed it would yield the type of excitement that Stern experienced.

Fenton was responsible for the production of many lessons used and adapted by teachers and students that enabled students to discover historical knowledge for themselves. One such lesson Fenton and some of his colleagues (Good et al., 1969) created involved the historical topic of nineteenth-century Russia and the roots of totalitarianism. In keeping with Fenton's style, the lesson used a *primary source* (a first-hand account of a historical event) as opposed to a textbook or another secondary source created by a historian. "Instead of an historian's explanation of the past," the authors asserted, "the students read portions of an English journalist's observations of Russian society at the end of the nineteenth century" (Good et al., 1969, p. 32). This reading included the journalist's description of a Russian village, his experience with a Russian family, and description of the political and economic life of Russia. Based on this reading, the authors provided questions for students to answer such as: What were the values of nineteenth-century Russians as revealed in Russian family life? How was the Russian economy organized? Teachers were then suggested to organize students into learning groups and have them form their own questions based upon social science concepts to analyze the journalist's account. Additionally, teachers were suggested by this lesson to ask the students the following question: "Can you make a hypothesis about the value system of Imperial Russia based upon these generalizations about the political, economic, and social system?" (Good et al., 1969, p. 33).

Fenton's work ebbed and flowed with source-based instruction much akin to what he shared in the Russian history exercise. In addition to primary documents, Fenton (1967) suggested teachers use data tables such as one that emphasized the gross national product of the United States over the span of the decade leading up to the Great Depression. These data would be used alongside a series of questions such as "What happened to GNP during the 1920s?" This line of questioning, in the spirit of the scientific method, always began with students formulating a hypothesis of their own. Fenton also advocated hypothesis formation based on source quotes, pictures, or sound recordings. In the wake of Fenton's emphasis on source-based instructional "revolution," companies began the production of curriculum materials fitting with this instructional approach. Perhaps the most prominent of these materials were the source-based packets created by *Jackdaws®* that many social studies teachers used throughout the 1970s. A visit to the Jackdaws® website (www.jackdaws.com) reveals the nature of these packets that can still be purchased today. Each packet is usually based on a particular historical theme or era in American history, or world history, and was filled with primary sources related to that theme or era. These packets, though rarely referred to today by teacher educators, are wonderful remnants of the new social studies' emphasis on source-based instruction where students were positioned to play the role of the social scientist. While the new social studies movement may have reached its zenith in 1967 and pervasively reappeared throughout the 1970s in the world of social studies education, its influence did not remain there alone. A contemporary surge of interest in source-based instruction demonstrates the "cyclical nature of efforts at school reform" (Evans, 2010, p. 31). We will now turn to this recent cycle of source-based instruction that is remarkably like Fenton's new social studies only with a different name: *historical thinking*.

Historical Thinking

The recent scholarship on historical thinking is one of the most significant breakthroughs in contemporary social studies education. While rarely associated with the new social studies movement of many decades ago, there is no mistaken the resemblance between historical thinking and Fenton's work on history teaching and learning. Put simply, historical thinking is a set of skills for interpreting and analyzing primary source documents for the purpose of constructing an account of the past. The individual primarily responsible for breathing new life into this new rendition of history teaching and learning is an educational psychologist from Stanford University named *Sam Wineburg* (b. 1958).

Three decades ago, Wineburg (1991) published a research study that compared the analytical processes of professional historians with those of advanced secondary students as each respective group encountered primary sources. The study yielded the significant finding that those professionally trained in history possessed a knowledge different from the untrained high school student of history:

> What seemed to distinguish historians from students was not whether they could identify Fort Ticonderoga or the Townsend Acts but broader, more sweeping ways of knowing and thinking about historical evidence . . . knowledge of how to establish warrant and determine the validity of competing truth claims in a discipline.
>
> (Wineburg, 1991, p. 84)

Critical analysis of primary sources, according to Wineburg, requires close examination of the author's intent, purpose, and techniques. This is opposed to a mere face-value acceptance of the claims of the author. Wineburg (2001) argued that history teachers would better serve students if they positioned students to engage in the disciplinary thinking that historians engage in.

Wineburg's articulation of the nature of disciplinary thinking among historians was popularized with the 2001 publication of his book *Historical Thinking and Other Unnatural Acts: Charting the Future of Teaching the Past* (Wineburg, 2001). By 2002, Wineburg's transition from the University of Washington to Stanford University led to the formation of the Stanford History Education Group (SHEG), a research and development group of Stanford faculty, staff, graduate students, and visiting scholars that sought to refine and implement historical thinking practices in school districts. SHEG's well-known website (www.sheg.stanford.edu) yields a bounty of curricular resources for history teachers. The four historical thinking skills that SHEG hones in on within the resources are: sourcing, corroboration, contextualization, and close reading. Table 7.1 provides a description of these four skills along with key questions SHEG crafted to help teachers develop these skills among students when using primary sources in their classroom. As you can see in Table 7.1, each of these skills focus on a different approach students may take with primary sources, including analyzing

Table 7.1 Historical Thinking Skills

Skill	Sourcing	Corroboration	Contextualization	Close Reading
Description	Asks students to consider who wrote a document as well as the circumstances of its creation.	Asks students to consider details across multiple sources to determine points of agreement and disagreement.	Asks students to locate a document in time and place and to understand how these factors shape its content.	Helps students evaluate sources and analyze rhetoric.
Key Questions	• Who wrote this? • What is the author's perspective? • Why was it written? • When was it written? • Where was it written? • Is this source reliable? Why? Why not?	• What do other documents say? • Do the documents agree? If not, why? • What are other possible documents? • What documents are most reliable?	• When and where was the document created? • What was different then? • What was the same? • How might the circumstances in which the document was created affect its content?	• What claims does the author make? • What evidence does the author use? • What language (words, phrases, images, symbols) does the author use to persuade the document's audience? • How does the document's language indicate the author's perspective?

Source: Stanford History Education Group: www.sheg.stanford.edu

the authorship of the source (sourcing), cross-comparison of a source with other sources (corroboration), identifying the historical context of the source (contextualization), and an in-depth analysis of the nature of the content of the source (close reading).

While Wineburg's work continued to grow in popularity among teachers and teacher educators in the United States, other scholars crafted a more comprehensive and nuanced conception of historical thinking. Chief among these scholars is *Peter Seixas* (b. 1947), professor of education at the University of British Columbia (UBC). While Seixas was born in New York City and went to college in Philadelphia, the entirety of Seixas' academic career was at UBC where he spearheaded a decades-long effort to reshape history teaching and learning in Canada. In sum, Seixas saw historical thinking as being more expansive than Wineburg's exclusive emphasis on inquiry with primary sources. Seixas (2015) saw Wineburg's conception of historical thinking in this way: "the methods of doing history became the ends of doing history" (p. 4). In turn, Seixas conceived of historical thinking through six key concepts: historical significance, evidence, continuity and change, cause and consequence, historical perspective taking, and ethical dimension (Seixas et al., 2013).

Table 7.2 shows each of Seixas' historical thinking concepts alongside a key question to clarify the nature of each concept. Seixas' concepts of "evidence" and "historical perspective taking" resonate well with Wineburg's list of historical thinking skills (see Table 7.1). However, "historical significance," "continuity and change," "cause and consequence," and "ethical dimension" possess characteristics that extend beyond Wineburg's emphasis on primary source analysis and toward a broader examination of the past. With that said, Seixas' conceptual model of historical thinking may fit nicely within the melioristic tradition promoted by Dewey, Rugg, and Alan Griffin. For instance, let's consider a lesson on the American Civil War. According to Seixas' conceptual model, the class should examine the "historical significance" of the American Civil War. That is best done by looking at the nature of civil war itself, necessitating the study of other civil wars alongside the American Civil War, including those from the past and

Table 7.2 Historical Thinking Concepts (Seixas et al., 2013)

Historical Thinking Concept	Key Questions
Historical Significance	What sort of change did the event, person, or development create?
Evidence	What inferences can be made from primary sources about the event, person, or development?
Continuity and Change	What changed and what remained the same as a result of the event, person, or development?
Cause and Consequence	What were the causes and consequences of the change created by the event, person, or development?
Historical Perspective Taking	What were the beliefs, values, and motivations of those in the past being studied?
Ethical Dimension	What informed judgements can be made about the event, person, or development?

the present. Since "historical significance" focuses on the nature of change brought forth from a particular event, the teacher may position students to explore the changes brought forth from the American Civil War alongside changes brought forth from other civil wars in history to determine if any generalizations might be able to be made (see Chapter 4 for more on generalizations). As a result, this generalization may be used to examine characteristics of contemporary society to determine if seeds of civil war may exist. This same process may occur regarding the concepts of "continuity and change" and "cause and consequence." A teacher may address the concepts of "evidence" and "historical perspective taking" by using Wineburg's model of historical thinking skills (i.e., sourcing, corroboration, contextualization, and close reading) within the lesson(s) by including personal letters, speeches, and policy documents such as the Emancipation Proclamation. In this way, the Wineburg and Seixas conceptions of historical thinking may complement one another quite nicely.

Disciplinary Thinking and Democratic Citizenship

There are numerous benefits of a disciplinary approach to teaching and learning. For one, its emphasis on inquiry promotes a kind of exploration that may excite students. The anecdote by Barbara Slater Stern about her sixth-grade experience testifies to this. Inquiry is also closely connected to the type of reflective thought that John Dewey (1933) emphasized in *How We Think*: "Active, persistent, and careful consideration of any belief or supposed form of knowledge in the light of the grounds that support it and the further conclusions to which it tends" (p. 118). Disciplinary thinking may require all the components of reflective thought: inference, evidence gathering, and a settled situation (Barton & Levstik, 2004). As a case in point, a student may be introduced to a lesson on the American Revolution by first reading *the Declaration of Independence*. That student may be asked by the teacher to read the document closely (see Table 7.1 for Wineburg's series of close reading questions). The answers to the close reading questions represent inferences (hypotheses) related to the document. Second, the teacher may require the student to examine other documents such as private letters or other political documents from the revolutionary war era. This kind of corroboration (see Table 7.1) represents a type of evidence gathering that helps students further examine their initial inferences. The student may therefore come to a settled situation about the American Revolution by making evidence-based claims that fit closely to Seixas' concepts of historical significance, historical perspective taking, and the ethical dimension. As was the case in Fenton's work, a balance of questioning and student self-discovery would be at play in such an activity that cultivated reflective thought. Third, while a disciplinary approach may cultivate reflective thought and source corroboration, it also has the potential to foster moral development among students. A key feature of this moral development that a disciplinary approach (particularly historical thinking) promises to nurture is through empathic development. Empathy "involves imagining the thoughts and feelings of other people from their own perspectives" (Barton & Levstik, 2004, p. 206). Social studies educators Keith Barton and Linda Levstik (2004) claimed that historical thinking positions a student to encounter other perspectives and requires them to seriously consider those perspectives. This perspective recognition is crucial for democratic deliberation since it counters any tendency one may have to dismiss others' perspectives as merely the result of "ignorance, stupidity, or delusion" (Barton & Levstik, 2004, p. 211). While empathetic development may foster perspective recognition, it may also help students to care for others (Barton & Levstik, 2004). While perspective recognition fits mostly as a cognitive characteristic, caring is an emotional characteristic that is equally important among a democratic citizenry. Care may come in the form of a feeling of sadness or remorse for an atrocity of the past such as the plight of Native Americans during the Trail of Tears, the treatment of Japanese Americans sent to internment camps during the Second World War, the dehumanization of African Americans through slavery and the era of Jim Crow, and the refusal to allow women to participate in public life. This sort of caring for others who are often marginalized is a fundamental building block for individuals to be able and willing to advocate for such marginalized populations when they encounter further discrimination. We will learn more about moral education, including caring, in our next chapter.

While a disciplinary approach to the social studies has numerous benefits, it does bring forth some concerns. Atop the list of concerns is that it may subjugate civic education to the realm of a particular discipline, such as history, as opposed to explicitly prioritizing civic education. If a teacher exclusively stresses the disciplinary practices of history, for instance, there may be little time left to explore contemporary issues. This was the focus of another prominent project called the Harvard Social Studies Project (HSSP) that also received federal funding in the era of the new social studies movement. The primary architects of HSSP, Donald Oliver, Fred Newmann, and James Shaver, became prominent figures in social studies education for their work on teacher education despite the modest impact the HSSP had upon schools (Francis, 2014). Their work emphasized what Oliver called a "jurisprudential" approach to teaching in that they sought to position students as judges of public policy issues considering evidence presented to them in a discussion-based format. We will look further at this approach in a later chapter.

Fenton's impact on schools exceeded that of HSSP. In an ideal educational setting, teachers would have the necessary time to thoroughly address disciplinary practices and follow through with a careful examination of related contemporary issues. However, classrooms cannot be provided such an ideal situation due to time constraints and other curricular priorities. Stressing the features of an academic discipline may have the effect of casting aside civic education as a key aim of the social studies classroom. We will see in a later chapter that social studies educator and former president of the National Council for the Studies (NCSS) Shirley Engle articulated this concern in his 1970 NCSS presidential address. Therefore, teachers should employ a disciplinary approach as an important pedagogical strategy for the social studies teacher as opposed to serving as the preeminent model for instruction as some of its advocates seem to push. It is important to remember that a social studies teacher needs to explicitly address the cultivation of the necessary knowledge, skills, and dispositions to perpetuate democratic life. A disciplinary approach may assist with this, but it alone cannot be solely relied upon by teachers to handle this important work.

Summary

In the late 1950s, the Soviet launching of Sputnik caused deep concern across the United States that the country was falling behind as a global superpower. To address this concern, the United States government spearheaded a comprehensive reform effort on teaching and learning in elementary and secondary schools. This paved the way for what became known as "the new social studies movement" where curriculum was crafted to privilege the disciplinary practices of the social sciences in classrooms. Historian Edwin Fenton rose to prominence during this reform movement with a robust effort to change the teaching and learning of history. Fenton emphasized what he called discovery learning where students relied less on the direction of teachers and were expended more leeway to explore historical topics on their own through primary source instruction. By the late 1960s and throughout the 1970s, Fenton's efforts fueled the rise and production of curricular materials that emphasized such primary source instruction. By the 1990s, the inquiry-based practices promoted by Fenton later resurfaced in the form of historical thinking. Historical thinking consists of the set of skills commonly used by professional historians to interpret and analyze primary source documents for the purpose of constructing an account of the past. Educational psychologist Sam Wineburg resuscitated Fenton's ideas of the new social studies into a fresh approach that promised to enliven history teaching and learning. Primarily due to

Wineburg's efforts, a plethora of research on historical thinking fueled the wide promotion of historical thinking as a central pedagogical path for history instruction across the country. While Wineburg's version of historical thinking focused primarily on analysis of primary source documents, history educator Peter Seixas provided a more comprehensive description of historical thinking that encompassed not only the analysis of primary source documents but also the evaluation and interpretation on what makes something historically significant, continuity and change as it relates with a particular event or circumstance, causes and consequences of a particular event, and an ethical judgement on the positive or negative impact of that particular event, person, or circumstance being studied. Seixas' approach to history teaching and learning allows for social meliorism, whereas Wineburg's approach does not coordinate as closely with it. A disciplinary approach to social studies education has numerous advantages and some disadvantages as an instructional strategy for social studies educators' larger effort to cultivate democratic citizenship among their students.

Reflective Exercises

1. What was "new" about the new social studies movement?
2. How do social and political events shape the teaching and learning of history? In what way(s) was the new social studies movement shaped by social and political events?
3. Compare and contrast the approaches of history teaching and learning promoted by Sam Wineburg with those promoted by Peter Seixas. Which do you prefer? Why?
4. Do you think that historical thinking is compatible or not compatible with social meliorism? Explain.

References

Barton, K. C., & Levstik, L. S. (2004). *Teaching history for the common good.* Routledge.

Bestor, A. (1953). *Educational wastelands: The retreat from learning in our public schools.* University of Illinois Press.

Bruner, J. (1960). *The process of education.* Harvard University Press.

Byford, J., & Russell, W. (2007). The new social studies: A historical examination of curriculum reform. *Social Studies Research and Practice, 2*(1), 38–48.

Cude, M. D. (2010). Can you still catch fish with the new social studies bait? Ted Fenton and the Carnegie-Mellon (Social Studies) Project. In B. S. Stern (Ed.), *The new social studies: People, projects, and perspectives* (pp. 75–94). Information Age Publishing, Inc.

82   *Disciplinary Thinking*

Dewey, J. (1933). *How we think: A restatement of the relation of reflective thinking to the educative process*. D.C. Heath & Co Publishers.

Evans, R. (2010). National security trumps social progress: The era of the new social studies in retrospect. In B. S. Stern (Ed.), *The new social studies: People, projects, and perspectives* (pp. 1–37). Information Age Publishing, Inc.

Fenton, E. (1967). *The new social studies*. Holt, Rinehart, and Winston, Inc.

Francis, A. T. (2014). Diffusing the social studies wars: The Harvard Social Studies Project 1957–1972. *American Educational History Journal, 41*(1/2), 373.

Good, J. M., Farley, J. U., & Fenton, E. (1969). Developing inquiry skills with an experimental social studies curriculum. *The Journal of Educational Research, 63*(1), 31–35.

Parker, W. C. (2003). *Teaching democracy: Unity and diversity in public life*. Teachers College Press.

Seixas, P. (2015). A model of historical thinking. *Educational Philosophy and Theory*, 1–13. https://doi.org/10.1080/00131857.2015.1101363

Seixas, P., Morton, T., Colyer, J., & Fornazzari, S. (2013). *The big six: Historical thinking concepts*. Nelson Education.

Stern, B. S. (2010). Introduction. In B. S. Stern (Ed.), *The new social studies: People, projects, and perspectives* (pp. xiii–xxii). Information Age Publishing, Inc.

Wineburg, S. (1991). Historical problem solving: A study of the cognitive processes used in the evaluation of documentary and pictorial evidence. *Journal of Educational Psychology, 83*(1), 73–87. https://doi.org/10.1037/0022-0663.83.1.73

Wineburg, S. (2001). *Historical thinking and other unnatural acts: Charting the future of teaching the past*. Temple University Press.

8 Morality

At the end of the school day, Madi left her classroom to retrieve something from her car. As she approached the stairs, she heard a loud THUMP above her. Rather than going downstairs as she planned, she went up to see what happened. Atop the stairs, she saw George Norton on the ground, his books scattered and with other students laughing at him as they hurried down the steps to leave home for the day.

"Are you OK, George?" Madi asked as she rushed to him. "Yeah, I'm fine. Jerks!" Madi picked up George's books and helped him up. George was one of Madi's first-period students. He struggled to fit in with his classmates, and this struggle sometimes put the worst of Middleborough on display. This afternoon was a perfect case in point.

An hour and a half later, after Madi finished grading papers and preparing for the next day, she had some time while driving home to think about George and what happened. As she arrived at her apartment and walked to her front-porch step, Madi knew she needed to do something as a flurry of thoughts rushed through her mind: "How can I get these kids to think of others? To be more kind to one another? They are so selfish sometimes!"

As 1926 rolled around, *Ernest Horn* (1882–1967) was fed up in much the same way as we just saw Madi Hobbs. Horn, a curriculum professor at the University of Iowa in the early mid-twentieth century, grew increasingly frustrated with the growing self-centeredness and general disregard for the public good in our country. He was bothered by such things as colleagues gladly accepting an honorarium for work they did not do and children trampling on neighbors' gardens as they walked home from school (Schul & Hamot, 2011). As a result, he gathered a sense of resolve and set out on a mission to change things through public education. First, he empowered his graduate students, many of whom were practicing teachers in Iowa, by teaching a course titled "Moral and Civic Education" where he used case situations to position students to consider others' perspectives and situations (Schul & Hamot, 2011). Second, during that same year, Horn (1926)

DOI:10.4324/9781003372318-8

published an essay entitled *Moral and Civic Education in the Elementary School* where he spelled out the problem and the prominent role public schools can play with addressing the problem. Horn, a hopeful optimist, believed that public education could be where society improved and people began to care for others and their democracy.

The problem, as Horn saw it, was not a unique one for societies. He called it *"romantic individualism"* and defined it as "self-expression apart from service, and freedom without responsibility" (Horn, 1926, p. 188). A contemporary take on the problem that Horn put his finger on is *Walter Parker's* articulation of *idiocy*. Parker (b. 1948), a social studies educator at the University of Washington, referenced the ancient Greeks' conception of idiocy as a general disregard for the betterment of the city-state:

> Idiot (idiotes) was a term of reproach in ancient Greece reserved for persons who paid no attention to public affairs and engaged in only self-interested or private pursuits, never mind the public interest – the civic space and the common good.
>
> (Parker, 2003, p. xv)

Those who disregard social responsibility in this way often do so in the name of preserving their individual liberty. This idea has actually gained popularity in the modern-day philosophy of libertarianism where its proponents often hail the mid-twentieth century writer and philosopher *Ayn Rand's* (1905–1982) idea of individual happiness and productive achievement serving as the primary aim of one's life. This philosophy prominently plays out in contemporary public policy initiatives such as the privatization of public education or curtails against environmental protections (MacLean, 2017; Mayer, 2016). We saw how this philosophy dangerously permeated across the electorate during the COVID-19 pandemic when cries for individual liberty for those who opposed mitigation strategies and vaccination usurped any notion of social responsibility. Neighborliness is protecting individuals. One's freedom is closely tied to the health of their community. "We are free so that we can create a community life," Walter Parker (2003) asserted, "so that, in turn, we can be free" (p. 4).

Morality is a system of principles and values that a society holds valuable for its health and stability. A democracy depends upon its citizenry to support it. This requires individuals to behave as citizens who harbor a sense of responsibility for their society. While public policy in the mid-twentieth century emphasized academic rigor in social studies education, some scholars contributed to the field in ways that represented a more expansive vision of education. These scholars emphasized morality as a central educational endeavor. To what extent is academic rigor valuable, these scholars argued, if schools are producing students who are immoral? In many ways, these scholars built upon the work initially laid out by John Dewey's articulation of a social democracy, which served as a guiding force for Ernest Horn's efforts nearly a century ago. These scholars, in sum, picked up where Dewey and Horn left off. This chapter focuses upon the work of the two most prominent of these scholars: Lawrence Kohlberg and Nel Noddings.

Lawrence Kohlberg

Lawrence Kohlberg (1927–1987) was a psychologist at the University of Chicago, and later Harvard University, who catapulted himself in the national spotlight with his groundbreaking dissertation while a graduate student at the University of Chicago. Completed in 1958, Kohlberg's dissertation featured a theory of moral development that became the basis for his entire career's work. His theory of moral development emphasized isolated instances of cognitive judgement as opposed to emotion or habitual behavior. A cognitive development approach was first articulated by John Dewey (1964), who first conceived of development through moral stages, and later expanded by psychologist *Jean Piaget* (1896–1980) who, in 1948, built on Dewey's theory on moral stages by empirically investigating them through interviewing and observing children (Piaget, 1948). Kohlberg built on this Dewey-Piaget work on moral stages to craft a clear and thorough theory of moral development based on longitudinal empirical research. Kohlberg's work provided a significant step for better understanding morality among individuals and how moral development could be addressed as an instructional goal in classrooms.

The primary means Kohlberg sought to cultivate morality among students in school was through stories involving moral dilemmas. Kohlberg believed that providing students an opportunity to navigate through a situation with a moral dilemma allows those students to develop their moral reasoning and judgement. The most famous of these dilemmas that Kohlberg (1958) used centered around a man he called Heinz. See Figure 8.1 for a common version of the *Heinz dilemma*.

Questioning was an important component of Kohlberg's process with using dilemmas. The goal of using this dilemma was to help identify and develop students' moral reasoning. Next is a list of questions like what he typically asked regarding the Heinz dilemma (McLeod, 2013):

- Should Heinz have stolen the drug?
- Would it matter if Heinz did not love his wife?
- Would it matter if the person dying was a stranger?
- Should the police arrest the chemist for murder if Heinz's wife died?

> *Heinz's wife was dying from a particular type of cancer. Doctors said a new drug might save her. The drug had been discovered by a local chemist, and Heinz tried desperately to buy some, but the chemist was charging ten times the money it cost to make the drug, and this was much more than Heinz could afford.*
>
> *Heinz could only raise half the money, even after help from family and friends. He explained to the chemist that his wife was dying and asked if he could have the drug cheaper or pay the rest of the money later.*
>
> *The chemist refused, saying that he had discovered the drug and was going to make money from it. The husband was desperate to save his wife, so later that night he broke into the chemist's laboratory and stole the drug.*

Figure 8.1 Heinz's Dilemma

Source: McLeod, S.A. (2013). Kohlberg. *Simply Psychology*. www.simplypsychology.org

Kohlberg used the Heinz dilemma and this line of questioning as a basis for his dissertation at the University of Chicago in the late 1950s. He used six dozen boys from Chicago, aged 10–16 years, with a vast majority (58 in total) of them followed up with in three-year intervals for 20 years where he used other dilemmas and related lines of questioning (Kohlberg, 1984; McLeod, 2013). This work resulted in the creation and refinement of Kohlberg's breakthrough theory of moral development (see Table 8.1).

According to Kohlberg's theory, there are three levels of moral development: pre-conventional, conventional, and post-conventional. At the pre-conventional level, most commonly, but not always, occupied by younger children, individuals' decisions are driven out of strict adherence to authority and/or fear of punishment. In this level, any inkling an individual may have that helps others is done so out of self-interest as opposed to altruism. At the conventional level, an individual's decisions are based primarily on societal norms. This level requires a level of role-playing or reciprocity between individuals – all based on social norms. For instance, if Heinz was a good husband, he would steal the drug. However, he would have to weigh that with a concern for where his theft may or may not contribute to a decay of social order. At the post-conventional level, individuals are motivated much more on universal principles as opposed to social norms. The overarching motivation for individuals' behavior at this mature level is truth and justice, regardless of legal or social consequences of the behavior. Kohlberg viewed these levels as stages of progression for individuals but with an understanding that not everyone may experience each level in their development.

Table 8.1 Kohlberg's Theory of Moral Development

Level of Moral Development	Focus of Interest	Description and Stages	Relationship to Heinz Dilemma
Pre-conventional	Self-Only Society	Behavior is based on obedience of authority and fear of punishment. Stage one: Obedience and Punishment Stage two: Individualism and Exchange	If caught, there is punishment. If not caught, Heinz's self-interest is satisfied.
Conventional		Behavior is based on societal norms. Stage three: Good Interpersonal Relationships Stage four: Maintaining Social Order	What would a good husband do for his wife? Stealing is illegal. Would stealing contribute to social disorder?
Post-conventional		Behavior is self-chosen and rooted solely on what is right and just. Stage five: Social Contract and Individual Rights Stage six: Universal Principles	The right to life versus property rights. What is right regardless of law?

Classroom Application: The Socratic Method

Kohlberg believed that teachers could engage students in discussion about ethical dilemmas to foster their stage development. He valued such moral discussion because he saw that it contained three important conditions:

1. Exposure to the next higher stage of reasoning.
2. Exposure to situations posing problems and contradictions for the child's current moral structure, leading to dissatisfaction with his current level.
3. An atmosphere of interchange and dialogue combining the first two conditions, in which conflicting moral views are compared in an open manner.

(Kohlberg, 1976)

These conditions became the basis for Kohlberg's optimism for the social studies classroom to become a literal laboratory for democratic development.

Kohlberg (1976) surmised that education in a democracy should focus on issues of morality and fairness first with small-group discussion followed by large democratic community meetings. He believed this was the best approach to develop individuals' higher-stage thinking.

The most effective type of moral discussion, according to Kohlberg (1976), was the *Socratic seminar*. Unlike typical discussions where teacher voices are prominent and indoctrination might appear, a Socratic seminar is a discussion that almost exclusively involves students. The only exception lies with the line of questioning, which is typically facilitated by the teacher. There are numerous ways of conducting Socratic seminars, but one simple approach is for the teacher to provide an ethical dilemma, such as the Heinz dilemma on Figure 8.1, to each student to quietly read for themselves. Once each student read the dilemma, the teacher may proceed by asking the class an initial question such as "Should Heinz have stolen the drug?" Since students are positioned to discuss with one another, it is often suggested that student desks be arranged in a circular fashion so students may see one another as they speak. While some advocates of Socratic seminars suggest that teachers may also be participants in the discussion, participation by the teacher should be minimized to ensure students have the intellectual freedom and space to think for themselves and with one another as they grapple with the questions related to the dilemma. Once conversation on a particular question appears to be dwindling in nature, the teacher should proceed with asking the following question (i.e., Would it matter if Heinz did not love his wife?). This format should continue for roughly 30 minutes, depending upon the nature of the discussion.

One of the key characteristics of a Socratic seminar is that it values student perspective. Teachers who take such a position are likely to care for their students and foster an environment where students care for one another. Kohlberg believed that cognitive development required such care and respect, but later moral educators placed a greater emphasis on care as a central theme to moral development. The next section focuses on the most prominent of these educators: Nel Noddings.

Nel Noddings and the Ethic of Care

While Kohlberg's theory of moral development gained in popularity and usefulness, it also received significant criticism. At the forefront of this criticism was its blatant sex bias brought forth most prominently by psychologist Carol Gilligan (b. 1936). Kohlberg's theory was based on empirical research, typical at the time, that exclusively focused on boys, and the Heinz dilemma centered on a male. The concern with such an emphasis on males is that justice for all served as Kohlberg's apex of moral reasoning when other options closely associated with feminine characteristics were available. At the forefront of these feminine characteristics are a care and concern for others (Gilligan, 1977). It is with this point that *Nel Noddings* (1929–2022) prominently laid a foundation for a paradigm of morality and moral education that enriches and challenges the work conducted by Kohlberg.

Nel Noddings' life and career is extraordinary. She was an elementary and high school teacher for 17 years prior to venturing into higher education after earning a PhD from Stanford University in the mid-1970s. She went on to join the Stanford faculty in 1977 where she grew to become a prominent philosopher of education. Noddings (1984) gained acclaim with the publication of her book *Caring: A Feminine Approach to Ethics and Moral Education*. It is worth noting that she dedicated this book to her husband, Jim, whom she lived an emotionally healthy and fulfilling life with for over 60 years. She and her husband raised ten children together with 39 grandchildren. With that said, Noddings' emphasis on the ethic of caring was done so out of immense integrity. She practiced what she taught.

In *Caring*, Noddings (1984) repudiated using a theoretical outlook on caring that included stage development. She was particularly concerned with Kohlberg's placement of good interpersonal relationships at a less advanced stage (stage three). Her concern arose because she perceived caring to be a feminine characteristic that placed higher value on interpersonal relationships as opposed to an abstract vision of justice. Noddings (1984) explained her perspective this way:

> But women, as ones-caring, are not so much concerned with the rearrangement of priorities among principles; they are concerned, rather, with maintaining and enhancing caring. They do not abstract away from the concrete situation those elements that allow a formulation of deductive argument; rather, they remain in the situation as sensitive, receptive, and responsible agents.
>
> (p. 42)

To Noddings, it is impossible to care in the abstract since it prerequisites a concrete relationship with another person. "One cares for something or someone," Noddings (1984) asserted, "if one has a regard for or inclination toward that something or someone" (p. 9). Caring, therefore, involves a relationship between at least two people: the "one-caring" and the cared for. Caring, therefore, requires the "one-caring" to have a certain dexterity in reading the emotional needs of others and how best to address those needs. "Even with those close to me," Noddings (1984) explained, "the intensity of caring varies; it may be calm and steady most of the time and desperately anxious in emergencies" (p. 16). This fluidity of concern for others that makes up the ethic of care, Noddings argued, requires an understanding of morality through concrete situations as opposed to hypothetical moral dilemmas. According to Noddings (1984), Kohlberg's theory of moral development does not take into consideration these points that are often associated as feminine characteristics:

> Women, perhaps the majority of women, prefer to discuss moral problems in terms of concrete situations. They approach moral problems not as intellectual problems to be solved by abstract reasoning but as concrete human problems to be lived and to be solved in living.
>
> (p. 96)

The point with bringing up Noddings' concerns with Kohlberg's theory is not to dismiss it altogether. To the contrary, Kohlberg provides social studies educators with a valuable framework and strategy to help address idiocy when it comes to democratic citizenship. However, Noddings also does that in a different manner through her emphasis on interpersonal and intrapersonal development. While Kohlberg perceived morality through reasoning, akin to Dewey and Piaget, Noddings looked at it through the emotional plane. Both can be useful, and, in fact, the complexities of morality may require both perspectives. While we already looked at how Kohlberg perceived moral education be taught through Socratic discussion, the next section focuses on ways Noddings viewed caring should be taught in the classroom.

Classroom Application: Caring in Schools

Noddings believed it was essential that our society approach education through a lens of caring. She saw the contemporary emphasis on academic content standards and high stakes standardized testing as a mistake packed with dire consequences. Atop these consequences is a neglect of teaching the skills and dispositions necessary for caring to take place. "When I care, I really hear, see, or feel what the other tried to convey," Noddings (2005) explained. These characteristics seldom come naturally and require explicit attention. Rather than a theoretical or hierarchical approach to moral education, Noddings believed that moral education required four components that teachers should possess: modeling, dialogue, practice, and confirmation. Figure 8.2 displays these components and what Noddings meant by each of them. Notice that these components require certain skills and dispositions of the teacher and is therefore reliant on interpersonal relationships between the teacher and students.

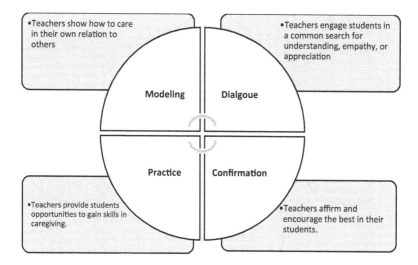

Figure 8.2 Noddings' Four Components of Moral Education
Source: Noddings (2005)

With modeling, Noddings believed teachers should demonstrate care with their own actions. Dialogue entails conversation between teachers and students about understanding, empathy, or appreciation of a particular person or thing. Teachers should also provide students opportunities to practice caring to equip students with skills in caregiving. Finally, teachers need to engage in confirmation of their students' best behavior as opposed to criticism of students' worst behavior. When put together, Noddings believed these four components foster a dynamic environment for a high-quality moral education to take place in schools.

While Noddings provided a pattern of behavior for teachers who desire to foster morality in their classroom, she also cast a curricular vision for schools that countered much of what contemporary educational policy and practice emphasizes. Figure 8.3 provides each theme of care that Noddings desired to see embedded in the school curriculum.

Each theme emphasizes a unique part of an individuals' life that they need to practice skills of caring. Atop Figure 8.3 is caring for self. To care for self requires attention to one's physical, mental, emotional, and spiritual life. Going clockwise in Figure 8.3 is caring in the inner circle. To care for those in an inner circle focuses on how individuals can and should cultivate relationships that are in close proximity such as family, friends, classmates, or colleagues. Next is caring for strangers and distant others. How should

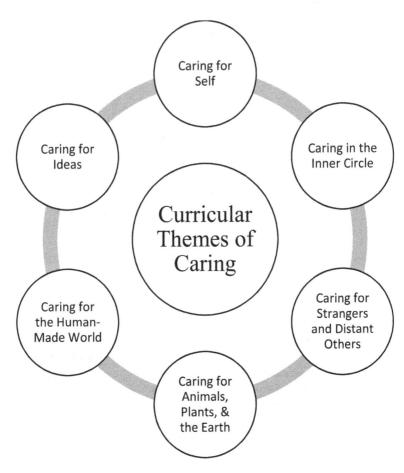

Figure 8.3 Noddings' Curricular Themes of Caring

Source: Noddings (2005)

an individual treat someone who is asking for directions? How should an individual speak or write to someone who may not be in their inner circle? Up next is caring for animals, plants, and the earth. Here, an individual learns to understand and appreciate other life forms such as animals and plants – as well as to properly tend to planet Earth. In this theme of care, the following questions should be highlighted: What are some characteristics of humane treatment of animals? Why is it important to treat animals humanely? How do plants support life on earth? How can individuals best tend to plants? How is the Earth affected by human behavior? What can individuals do to better take care of the Earth? The next theme of care is to care for the human-made world. Here, individuals are to better understand and appreciate synthetic creations in areas such as architecture, technology, or engineering. This also includes institutional creations such as democratic rule of law, political checks and balances, or due process. Finally, Noddings claimed that schools should teach students to care for ideas. To care for ideas may mean to value a liberal arts education that may help individuals better appreciate ideas in areas such as mathematics or art. This latter theme emphasizes a general concern for knowledge and beauty.

Noddings understood a curriculum that emphasizes caring is, in some respects, counterintuitive to the traditional school curriculum. She advocated for such things as more responsibility for teachers and students to exercise judgement, the elimination of competitive grading, and to encourage teachers to explore with students as opposed to playing the role of an all-knowing sage. As a result, society may push back on an emphasis on caring as being less rigorous than a curriculum that can be easily measured with a singular standardized test. To this notion, Noddings (2005) made her point clear: "Be clear and unapologetic about our goal. The main aim of education should be to produce competent, caring, loving, and loveable people" (p. 174).

Ernest Horn: A Fusion of Kohlberg and Noddings

While both Kohlberg and Noddings provided us with a clear and well-circulated vision for how teachers may best address issues of morality in their classroom, they were not the first to advocate for their approach. While neither referenced him in their work, Iowa's Ernest Horn put forth a vision decades earlier that resembled much of what Kohlberg and Noddings promoted. For instance, in 1926, Ernest Horn outlined an approach to moral education that also emphasized moral modeling on behalf of the teacher as well as dialogue and practice (Schul & Hamot, 2011). Horn suggested that teachers should provide students with a concrete situation that students could relate with. The next example is one of the situations that Horn used in a course he taught in 1926 at the University of Iowa titled *Moral and Civic Education* (Schul & Hamot, 2011):

> Mr. Middleton had $11 in the bank. He went to the bank one day, wrote a check for $10, and presented it at the cashier's window for the money. The cashier made a mistake and gave him $100.

> A. Was it Mr. Middleton's duty to tell the cashier of the error at once?
> B. Should he take the money and go out on the street to think it over?
> C. If Mr. Middleton decided to keep the money, should he be sent to the penitentiary?

Notice how similar the situation is to one of Kohlberg's dilemmas. Horn stressed that teachers should provide such situations to students, provide them the space to reflect on the situation, allow them to assess the situation, and then help guide the students to a resolution of the situation and connect it to any universal principles that the resolution may be connected to. Horn also provided an example to illustrate how he thought teachers should address moral situations with students where a first-grade teacher in a city of 40,000 people witnessed her students cutting across and damaging gardens on their way to school. Instead of lecturing to her students, she took the students to the recently damaged gardens and asked a series of questions, which positioned the students to view the situation from the perspective of the garden's owners. The students proceeded to discuss a plan, stop their current behavior, and began to instruct others on the matter (Schul & Hamot, 2011). This is like Noddings' components of modeling, dialogue, practice, and confirmation. This also fits a similar pattern of reflective inquiry advocated by John Dewey and Alan Griffin that we learned about in earlier chapters.

Horn's plan for moral education, though not identical to the ideas promoted by Kohlberg and Noddings, did possess key elements of the visions of both. Horn's plan helps us to see that Kohlberg and Noddings do not necessarily need to be looked at dualistically but can be complimentary. Kohlberg developed and advocated for a theory of moral development that says people pass through a series of stages. On the other hand, Noddings asserted that educators should be less concerned with stage development but with whether students have the skills and capacity to care for the person or thing they are with at the moment. In other words, Noddings prioritized interpersonal relationships, whereas Kohlberg emphasized universal justice as a primary aim for moral education. Whether one is more right than the other can be an important exercise, but both address the concerns that Walter Parker raised regarding idiocy within a democracy. Both Kohlberg and Noddings advocated for a position that requires individuals to be mature citizens who are concerned for others and their society. The blowing winds of self-centeredness find no home within individuals who are educated to cultivate a society focused on helping others.

Summary

A democracy depends upon its citizenry to share a concern for its well-being. Since a democracy entails a culture where individuals are concerned for others and the common good, it should be a curricular concern for schools that democratic education include a cultivation of morality. Morality is a system of values and beliefs that a society holds valuable for its health and stability. While moral education has been a concern throughout the history of social studies education, shown brightly through the works of John Dewey and Ernest Horn, two scholars in the mid-late twentieth century dedicated their careers to fostering a curricular emphasis on moral education in schools. These scholars, Lawrence Kohlberg and Nel Noddings, articulated visions of moral education that both complimented one another as well as starkly contrasted with one another. Both desired to see individuals develop a deep concern for others and their society. However, Kohlberg developed a theory of moral development with stages that climaxed toward a pinnacle of universal principles of truth and justice. He saw value in exposing students to hypothetical moral dilemmas where teachers may guide students' moral decision making through means such as discussion and a Socratic seminar. Noddings, on the other hand, focused on an earlier stage (conventional) that she believed Kohlberg merely glossed over as being less important than later stages. This conventional stage that drew the interest of Noddings emphasized interpersonal relationships. Noddings stressed that caring for self, others, and things should play a primary role in the development of individuals' morality.

Reflective Exercises

1. Look at Kohlberg's Heinz dilemma in Figure 8.1. Answer the following questions for yourself:

    - Should Heinz have stolen the drug?
    - Would it matter if Heinz did not love his wife?
    - Would it matter if the person dying was a stranger?
    - Should the police arrest the chemist for murder if Heinz's wife died?

2. After answering the questions associated with the Heinz dilemma, at what stage do you think you may be currently at on Kohlberg's theory of moral development (Figure 8.1)? Explain.

3. Do you agree with Noddings that we should prioritize interpersonal relationships (conventional stage in Kohlberg's theory of moral development) in moral education? Explain.

4. How can teachers best develop both moral reasoning and caring among their students?

References

Dewey, J. (1964). What psychology can do for the teacher. In R. Archambault (Ed.), *John Dewey on education: Selected writing*. Random House.

Gilligan, C. (1977). In a different voice: Women's conceptions of self and of morality. *Harvard Educational Review*, *47*(4), 481–517.

Horn, E. (1926). Moral and civic education in the elementary school. *The Annals of the American Academy of Political and Social Science, 125,* 187–192.

Kohlberg, L. (1958). The development of modes of thinking and choices in years 10 to 16 [Ph.D. Dissertation]. University of Chicago.

Kohlberg, L. (1976). The cognitive-developmental approach to moral education. In D. Purpel & K. Ryan (Eds.), *Moral education . . . it comes with the territory* (pp. 176–195). McCutchan.

Kohlberg, L. (1984). *The psychology of moral development: The nature and validity of moral Stages (essays in moral development, volume 2).* Harper & Row.

MacLean, N. (2017). *Democracy in chains: The deep history of the radical right's stealth plan for America.* Penguin.

Mayer, J. (2016). *Dark money: The hidden history of the billionaires behind the rise of the radical right.* Anchor.

McLeod, S. A. (2013). Kohlberg. *Simply Psychology.* www.simplypsychology.org

Noddings, N. (1984). *A feminine approach to ethics and moral education.* University of California Press.

Noddings, N. (2005). *The challenge to care in schools* (2nd ed.). Teachers College Press.

Piaget, J. (1948). *The moral judgment of the child* (2nd ed.). Free Press.

Schul, J., & Hamot, G. (2011) An engaged pragmatist: Uncovering and assessing Ernest Horn's view of moral education. *The Journal of Social Studies Research, 35*(2), 277–298.

9   Reclamation

"I'd like to have a vanilla ice cream cone dipped with butterscotch, please." Madi loved ice cream, and she loved the fact that she lived next to a pizza and ice cream carryout. She walked out of the carryout with her friend, Sarah, and they both sat on the picnic table adjacent to the parking lot. The two talked about their work, church activities, guys their friends wanted to set them up with, and the latest R & B music. Amidst one of these conversations, Madi noticed a car pulling away from the carryout. In the back seat was Michael, one of the seniors in her American Government class. Michael had a smirk on his face and gently waved goodbye to Madi as the car drove away. Madi reciprocated the wave along with the bright smile she was well known for.

A flurry of thoughts about Michael raced in her mind as she sat with Sarah. They only took a few moments, but they were rich and deep. Michael was a student who struggled in school, and Madi spent extra time with him outside of class. Michael wanted to be a plumber, and he failed to see the meaning in school. "Dr. Ellsworth was so right when he told our methods class that it isn't our business to train historians," she thought to herself. "It is our business, however, to prepare ordinary people for citizenship." Michael did not aspire to college life nor a white-collar career. "That smile meant a lot to me," Madi thought. "He didn't like school, but he must feel like he belongs in my class."

"Hey, Madi. Are you there?"

"Sorry, Sarah. I just saw someone I know and was thinking about them."

"Does your mom prod into your personal life? Mine does."

Madi laughed. "Yes. I guess that's what moms do."

The tradition of social meliorism took a back seat in the mid-late twentieth century to an increased interest in the social science disciplines. The work on moral education provided clues that school was more than academic preparation but a preparation for life and for a belonging to a democratic society that relied upon active participation from its citizenry. While

DOI:10.4324/9781003372318-9

helpful, the new social studies failed to provide answers to anything that did not focus on academic preparation for students. No one was more critical of this fact than *Shirley Engle* (1907–1994) of Indiana University. This chapter focuses on Engle's long-standing attempt to resuscitate social meliorism and reflective inquiry back into the field of social studies education.

Shirley Engle's career could serve as a blueprint for a model teacher educator. Engle was born in Illinois, went to college at the University of Illinois for both his undergraduate and graduate degrees, and served as a high school social studies teacher in Illinois schools for 17 years. In 1945, eight years before earning his PhD from the University of Illinois, Engle was hired by Indiana University to work in its teacher preparation program. This is where Engle worked for the remainder of his career, spanning a total of 31 years in academia. Engle's accolades are numerous, including serving as president of the National Council for the Social Studies (NCSS). His career can be seen as a continuation of Dewey, Griffin, Rugg, Hunt, and Metcalf. He believed that citizenship should remain the heart of social studies education with an emphasis on decision making.

Social Science Vs. Social Studies

A theme in Engle's work is his determination to revitalize the ancestral roots of social studies education as a field dedicated to cultivating democratic citizenship. In 1970, Engle was the president of NCSS and, as is customary for the president, addressed the membership at the annual NCSS meeting. Engle's speech was presented in New York City on November 20, 1970. He used the opportunity to defend the field of social studies education away from those forces he saw that detracted it away from the cultivation of democratic citizenship.

"We have 'Brunerized' the subjects and made inquiry our god," Engle (1970, p. 18) declared to the audience. Engle's reference to Jerome Bruner and inquiry was pinpointed directly to the new social studies movement, of which Engle was no fan. At the crux of Engle's frustration with the new social studies was how it skirted away from democratic citizenship, replacing it with an emphasis on the academic disciplines. "The so-called 'new' Social Studies of the'60s," Engle (1970) surmised, "while laudably embracing the principle of inquiry over that of rote memory in teaching the Social Sciences, has largely skirted or ignored the question of the ethical component of citizenship education" (p. 18). He referenced the 1916 Report from the NEA Committee on the Social Studies as the ancestral origins of the field of social studies education and that it defined the ethical component of citizenship education as the central purpose of the field:

> The Committee declared that the conscious and constant purpose of the Social Studies is the cultivation of good citizenship. The Committee

further declared the good citizen to be one who appreciates the nature of laws of social life, one who has an intelligent and genuine loyalty to high national ideals, one who has a sense of the responsibility of the individual as a member of social groups, one who is characterized by a loyalty and a sense of obligation to his city, state, nation, and to the human race, and one who has the intelligence and the will to participate effectively in the promotion of the social well-being. The Committee defined the Social Studies as all subject matter relating directly to the organization and development of human society and to man as a member of social groups.

(Engle, 1970, pp. 15–16)

As we saw in our previous chapter on morality, the ethical component of civic education typically takes a back seat to other aims that policy makers desire for schools to place their focus upon, namely academic and vocational preparation. However, Engle was not widening his critique about education policy writ large. Instead, Engle focused on the singular field of social studies education. While other factors may drive the purpose of the school, Engle boldly claimed democratic citizenship should serve as the centerpiece of social studies education. Engle believed that the new social studies movement was off course on this endeavor. According to Engle (1970), the social scientist is not concerned with democratic citizenship: "The social scientist has never claimed citizenship as his goal" (p. 23). Social scientists, according to Engle (1970), are primarily concerned with the scientific bent of their craft that is observable and measurable and less concerned with social problems that usually require reflective thinking.

Engle believed that social science played a crucial, yet subservient, role in social studies education. While social science produces knowledge, social studies education is "an applied field which attempts to fuse scientific knowledge with ethical, philosophical, religious, and social considerations which arise in the process of decision-making as practiced by the citizen" (Engle, 1970, p. 18). Engle (1970) did not intend to undermine the value of social science in his statement but put social science in its rightful place as a valuable and necessary tool for social studies educators:

In contrast to Social Science, the goal of Social Studies is the development of good citizens. The primary concern of Social Studies is the utilization of knowledge. The aim is to improve the process by which citizens use knowledge from the Social Sciences *and other sources* in making decisions concerning their individual behavior, and concerning questions of public policy.

(p. 21)

Therefore, Engle saw social science serving social studies education, not vice versa. He believed that the new social studies movement had flipped the table and laid the groundwork for a field where social science reigned supreme. It is in this spirit that Engle emphasized decision making as the heart of social studies education since it requires individuals to combine scientific knowledge with their own values to postulate on social issues.

Decision Making

In 1960, Shirley Engle (2003) published an article entitled *Decision Making: The Heart of Social Studies Instruction*. It is regarded as a seminal work in the field and lauded as one of the clearest and most succinct statements in support of reflective inquiry (Evans, 2004). Engle (2003) began the article with a simple declaration: "My theme is a very simple one. It is that, in teaching the social studies, we should emphasize decision making as against mere remembering" (p. 7). He sought to improve the level of intellectual activity in classrooms with the overall goal to improve intellectual activity in public life. Rather than engage in a "ground-covering" approach where teachers inundate students with a plethora of information, Engle (2003) strongly advised teachers to provide students with information alongside opportunities to pause and "speculate as to the meaning or significance of the material, or to consider its relevance and bearing to any general idea or to consider its applicability to any problem or issue past or present" (p. 8). In sum, Engle desired students use information presented before them to answer social issues in the classroom. There is a similarity between Engle's decision-making approach and the jurisprudential approach promoted by *Donald Oliver* (1929–2002), *Fred Newmann* (b. 1937), and *James Shaver* (b. 1933) during the era of the 1960s. Oliver, Newmann, and Shaver were prominent figures from the new social studies movement who, unlike Edwin Fenton, looked upon classroom discussion of public issues as a means to cultivate a meaningful civic education for students. As mentioned in an earlier chapter, they believed that teachers should position students as judges of public policy issues considering evidence presented to them via classroom discussion. This work culminated in the Harvard Social Studies Project that produced a wide selection of curricular pamphlets aimed to "encourage students to understand differing perspectives, evaluate, make judgements, and clarify values which are all ideas that represent the apex of human thinking" (Bohan & Feinberg, 2008, p. 62).

Engle, akin to Oliver, Newmann, and Shaver, emphasized that teachers should not engage students in rote learning but should position students to make decisions in class and to reflect on values held that paved the way for those decisions. "Real life decisions are ultimately value decisions," Engle

(2003, p. 10) surmised. Engle (2003) asserted that any policy decision an individual makes reflects values held by that individual:

> To duck the question of values is to cut the heart out of decision making. The basic social problem of America today is a problem of value. In simple terms the problem may be stated as to whether we value more the survival of a free America which will require sacrifice for education, for materials of defense, etc., or whether we value more our right as individuals to spend our resources on extra fins for our cars and for all the other gadgets of conspicuous consumption.
>
> (p. 10)

As Engle surmised, an individual's values are behind their decision making. For instance, if one looks at the 2020 election in the United States and the piles of data that support the conclusion that Joe Biden won the presidency, a person who values rule of law, peaceful transfer of power, and constitutional authority will reach the decision that Biden won. Of course, if one's values are primarily rooted in tribal affiliation in support of the incumbent, their confirmation bias led them to reach a different decision. Therefore, the contestation behind the 2020 election was really an issue over values. Similarly, the issue of climate change is supported by a plethora of data that points to the damage that humanity is wreaking on the environment. A decision to take measures to limit greenhouse gas emissions involves values centered around a responsible stewardship for the health of the environment. A decision to not take such a measure may involve values centered around economic prosperity and job security.

To engage students in *values clarification*, or self-awareness of how values may play a role in decisions and lifestyle choices, Engle believed that individuals should be provided opportunities to use knowledge as opposed to being delivered information for the purpose of committing it to memory. One useful resource where teachers can engage students in knowledge through decision making is National Issues Forums® (NIF). Created through the Kettering Foundation, a nonpartisan research foundation, NIF publishes a series of issue guides intended for groups to engage on policy deliberation. A look at NIF's website (www.nifi.org) reveals its bounty of issue guides community groups or schools may purchase. Each issue guide focuses on a contemporary issue that includes information about the issue. At the conclusion of each issue guide is a line of questioning participants are to answer, many of which require individuals to reflect on their values that may influence their decisions. Table 9.1 displays some recent NIF issue guide themes along with the line of questioning included in the guides. Under the left column of Table 9.1 is the title of the issue provided in the

Table 9.1 National Issues Forum® Questions and Values

Issue	Questions	Values
COVID-19 and Vaccines: How Should We Keep Our Communities Safe?	How much should we change our lives to adapt to the virus? What responsibilities does each of us have to our neighbors? How should we weigh the community's health against the need for more people to go back to work? How much weight do we put on reaching consensus and avoiding the controversies and divisions that may emerge?	Individualism Community Health Economic Prosperity Peace
Elections: How Should We Encourage and Safeguard Voting?	Would having uniform national standards for voting, instead of having state and local officials continue to set the rules, give us more confidence? Do ID requirements for voting, in order to help maintain the system's integrity, merely discourage voters by placing hurdles in their way? Would Americans see the voting system as more legitimate if the Electoral College were eliminated in favor of a national popular vote? Could some of the changes proposed here have unintended consequences? Could they fix some problems but cause new ones we haven't anticipated?	Election Integrity Election Participation Democratic Representation Political Power

Source: www.nifi.org

issue guide. The middle column are the questions provided in the issue guide intended for deliberation in various group settings once participants finished reading the background information on the issue.

The column on the right are values that may be associated with an individual's decisions on the policy related to the issue. For instance, individuals may firmly value individualism when refusing to accept any mandates as they relate to vaccines or masks. To these individuals, such mandates may be perceived as restrictions on their individualism. On the other hand, other individuals may firmly value community health or economic prosperity when advocating for vaccine or mask mandates as the surest way to protect community members and restore the economy back to health. An individual who may seek to offer individual choice to vaccination or masks may value peace in an environment fraught with tension over this issue. Such peace-seeking individuals may desire to appease others with the hope that the tension and disagreement goes by the wayside. Regardless of the position, values are at the core of an individual's decision making and questioning in the NIF issues guide fit Engle's approach quite well.

Socialization and Countersocialization

In 1988, Engle partnered with another professor of social studies education at Indiana University, *Anna Ochoa* (1933–2013), to write the book *Education for Democratic Citizenship: Decision Making in the Social Studies*. The book is regarded by many to be a classic in the field. In it, Engle and Ochoa persistently advocated for social studies education to focus on democratic citizenship and spelled out how that should be done. They were adamant that a democratic citizen must be both skilled and responsible as a decision maker. The book spelled out what such skills might look like, such as "being able to size up a problem and identify the real point of conflict of the real issue, including the underlying values that are at stake" (Engle & Ochoa, 1988, p. 25). Intellectual honesty was a tenet of their sense of responsibility citizens must possess since objectivity among individuals was necessary for the perpetuation of democratic life over society's natural impulse toward tribalism and authoritarianism. Much of these areas of emphasis had been loudly touted in the past, most notably through the work of John Dewey. Engle and Ochoa's most significant contribution to the front of this type of democratic education was their emphasis on a balanced education that would yield skilled and responsible democratic citizens.

Engle and Ochoa recognized that a healthy democratic society needed to balance liberty with conformity. They explained this conundrum:

> The task of educating citizens for a democracy presents a challenging and persistent dilemma. On the one hand, a democratic society is dedicated to promoting the exercise of liberty, which entails respect for diversity – politically, culturally, and intellectually. On the other hand, all societies, whether democratic or not, need to establish some degree of consensus and conformity among their citizens.
>
> (Engle & Ochoa, 1988, p. 28)

Engle and Ochoa proposed that to achieve this balance between liberty and conformity, individuals should be educated in such a way where they are

Table 9.2 Juxtaposition of Socialization and Countersocialization (Engle & Ochoa, 1988)

	Socialization	Countersocialization
Definition	"the process of learning the existing customs, traditions, rules, and practices of a society" (Engle & Ochoa, 1988, p. 29).	"the process of expanding the individual's ability to be a rational, thoughtful, and independent citizen of a society" (Engle & Ochoa, 1988, p. 29).
Characteristics	A conserving process with an emphasis on tradition. Strengthens social cohesiveness. Is doctrinaire, not reflective. Does not encourage individuals to think, analyze, and/or defend views with reason and evidence.	A learning process that fosters independent thought. Promotes reasoning and a reappraisal of what has been socialized.
Age/School Level	Emphasized in elementary schools "Yet in spite of the fact that some efforts at countersocialization can take place during the early grades, the socialization process will prevail in shaping the early values, attitudes, and behavior of young children" (Engle & Ochoa, 1988, p. 32).	Begin earnestly in late elementary and early middle school years "there can be no justification for the continuation of socialization practices during the adolescent years" (Engle & Ochoa, 1988, p. 32).

both socialized and countersocialized. *Socialization* and *countersocialization* are two concepts central to Engle and Ochoa's proposal for education for democratic citizenship. Table 9.2 juxtaposes these two concepts, with definition, characteristics, and appropriate age/school level provided for each concept to take place.

The top horizontal row of Table 9.2 provides Engle and Ochoa's definitions of socialization and countersocialization. Socialization refers to the learning of existing customs for the sake of a sense of conformity to a common set of ideals and customs. Characteristics (second horizontal row of Table 9.2) include a strengthening of social cohesiveness through a doctrinaire approach. This is typically practiced most prominently at the elementary school level. An example of this might come in the form of a practice such as reciting the Pledge of Allegiance or learning subject matter that might involve a celebration of the Fourth of July or learning a sense of reverence for heroes of the United States such as George Washington or Abraham Lincoln. Countersocialization, on the other hand, stresses reflective thought and, as a result, includes a questioning and reappraisal of what had been socialized. This is typically first practiced most prominently in the late elementary and early middle school years.

Engle and Ochoa (1988) emphasized that socialization had no place in the secondary level and that some forms of countersocialization, mainly through questioning, should be introduced at the elementary level. Some forms of countersocialization appropriate at the elementary level might involve something like how we define a family. Engle and Ochoa (1988) elaborated on this example:

> For example, children may learn about the family in a monolithic and narrow fashion. That is, they may learn that a family consists of a mother, father, and one or more children. As a result, they are likely to learn that alternative family arrangements (a single parent with a child, an older sister with a young child, etc.) are somewhat peculiar and are not seen as "real" families. In contrast, from a more diverse and broader perspective, children can also learn that families can and do take many viable forms.
>
> (pp. 35–36)

The goal of countersocialization, or democratic socialization as Engle and Ochoa also called it, is to promote democratic habits of mind such as diversity and reflective thought. This example of family definitions is an example of countersocialization that promotes such democratic values. At the secondary level, such opportunities for "democratic socialization" are boundless primarily due to the age of the student and nature of the subject matter. In a high school United States history course, for instance, a teacher might teach a unit on slavery that asks students such questions as "What impact has slavery had on our society?" or "One result of the Civil War is that slavery was no longer legal. Does the abolition of slavery justify the use of violence? Why?" (Engle & Ochoa, 1988, pp. 42–43). A teacher in a United States government course might have students critique the United States Constitution by comparing the American system of separation of powers with a parliamentary system where such a separation does not necessarily take place. A teacher may ask the students whether they believed the founders' plan of government was, indeed, the best possible plan. Such a question might be shocking to an individual who has been exclusively socialized that the American system of government is perfect. However, such a question is important for individuals to reflectively confront if they are to better understand their country's system of government and dynamics that occur where the checks and balances may help or hinder progress on policy. Calling something into question is the only way to better understand it and improve the situation at hand. Never questioning that thing leads to never fully understanding it and thus, not being equipped to improve the situation.

Engle and Ochoa stressed that teaching reflective thought is essential in education for democratic citizenship. They emphasized that classrooms must have a certain learning environment to successfully teach reflective thought. This learning environment, according to Engle and Ochoa (1988), involves: 1) an open and supportive classroom climate; 2) an emphasis on listening; 3) an environment where the teacher restates student ideas as opposed to consistently evaluate student comments; 4) an offering of competing ideas; 5) humor; and 6) the teacher as a model of reflective thought. These classroom characteristics closely resemble those characteristics that Hunt and Metcalf stressed were necessary to open closed areas. The resemblance between the ideas of Engle and Ochoa and those stressed decades earlier by Hunt and Metcalf are not a coincidence. They both prioritized democratic citizenship as central to social studies education.

Summary

As social policy and new educational initiatives shaped social studies education toward a pedagogy that emphasized the social science disciplines, Shirley Engle took a public and persistent stance toward reclaiming democratic citizenship as the central purpose of social studies education. He emphasized that decision making should play a prominent role in social studies classrooms, with an emphasis on a reflection of the values involved in individuals' decision making. In the late 1980s, Engle partnered with Anna Ochoa to write the book, *Education for Democratic Citizenship*, that clearly articulated this vision along with many other features that are now viewed as central practices in social studies education such as balancing socialization with countersocialization for the purposes of promoting a healthy democratic society that is both united but also stresses democratic liberty and reflective thought.

Reflective Exercises

1. What are the differences between being a "social studies teacher" as opposed to a "social science teacher"?
2. What is the purpose of school? What values are involved in your decision?

3. Describe some ways you have been socialized and countersocialized in your own educational experience.
4. Explain how Shirley Engle's position on social studies education is similar or different to the following individuals' positions we have examined in previous chapters:

- John Dewey
- Alan Griffin
- Harold Rugg
- Lawrence Kohlberg

References

Bohan, C. H., & Feinberg, J. (2008). The authors of the Harvard social studies project: A retrospective analysis of Donald Oliver, Fred Newmann, and James Shaver. *Social Studies Research and Practice, 3*(2), 54–67. https://www.socstrpr.org.

Engle, S. H. (2002). Exploring the meaning of the social studies. In M. A. Previte & J. J. Sheehan (Eds.), *The NCSS presidential addresses, 1970–2000: Perspectives on the social studies* (Vol. II). National Council for the Social Studies. (Original work published 1970)

Engle, S. H. (2003). Decision making: The heart of social studies instruction. *The Social Studies, 94*(1), 7–10.

Engle, S. H., & Ochoa, A. (1988). *Education for democratic citizenship: Decision making in the social studies*. Teachers College Press, Teachers College, Columbia University.

Evans, R. W. (2004). *The social studies wars: What should we teach the children?* Teachers College Press.

10 Infusion

A sense of excitement, nervousness, and closure is in the air today. As the graduates paraded in their caps and gowns, Madi looked upon them with joy and sadness at the same time. The joy comes from seeing them succeed and moving forward in life. The sadness comes with losing them as her students.

But, in another sense, they will always remain her students. She thought to herself about this notion as they climbed upon the stage and onto their chairs: "Each of these students are going into a world that is increasingly diverse, interconnected, and technologically changing at a rapid pace." The ceremony was beautiful. The families were excited. It was now time to greet the graduates in the outside procession line.

As Madi approached the students, a tap came upon her right shoulder. It was Mia Shubert, one of the students in her global studies course. "Ms. Hobbs," Mia said with tears running down her face, "thank you for this year. You've meant a lot to me." "You're welcome, Mia. You've meant a lot to me too." Two women approached Mia and Madi. "This is my mom and her partner, Sally. Mom, Sally, this is Ms. Hobbs. She's the best!" The four women greeted each other, discussed Mia's plans after high school, and pondered together about life in general. This conversation signaled to Madeline Elizabeth Hobbs of a job well done in her first year as a social studies teacher. There will be many more to come.

While the theme of reflective inquiry permeates throughout the historical and contemporary landscape of social studies education, new emphasis areas regularly emerge among scholars and practitioners in the field. As the twentieth century closed and we jettisoned through the first two decades of this century, three areas prominently emerged in social studies education that strengthened the field and improved its commitment toward democratic citizenship: multiculturalism, global education, and technology integration. These three areas are not intended to stand alone as a replacement of anything in the trajectory of social studies education but rather, are intended to

DOI:10.4324/9781003372318-10

enhance and enrich curricular practices. Therefore, we will classify these three areas as ones to be "infused," or pervasively included, throughout the social studies curriculum. In other words, these three areas should be naturally included throughout courses and projects in the field.

We will first look at multiculturalism by emphasizing the important work of James Banks. We will then focus on global education by first examining the perspective of M. Eugene Gilliom, one of the pioneers in the area, and then examining a recent NCSS position statement on global and international education in social studies. Finally, we will explore technology integration in the social studies by first looking at a seminal article on the topic crafted by Peter Martorella, then examining the framework of Technological and Pedagogical Content Knowledge.

Multiculturalism

The United States of America is a *pluralistic democracy*. This means that its population consists of a myriad of cultural differences related to themes such as race, national origin, sex, or gender. This runs contrary to a society that may have a monolithic population in any of the aforementioned areas. As a case in point, the United States is much more racially diverse than Finland. As a result of its diversity and commitment to democratic equality, education for citizenship in the United States must reflect the cultural characteristics of all students. This is the nature of *multiculturalism*.

The individual who had the greatest influence on the area of multiculturalism is *James Banks* (b. 1941) of the University of Washington. In fact, he is frequently referred to as the "father of multiculturalism" (Clabough & Clyde, 2021). Banks' career in education started in Chicago as a fifth-grade teacher before he became the first African American professor in the College of Education at the University of Washington by the early 1970s. Banks made an immediate impact on the field of social studies education through his scholarly and service efforts. In 1982, Banks was elected as the president of the National Council for the Social Studies, the first African American to hold that post. In his presidential address, Banks stressed the importance of balancing assimilationist forces with diversification in the education of the American citizenry. First, he spelled out why it is important for educators to be committed to understanding the diverse nature of their student population:

> Educators need to develop a sophisticated understanding of the diverse groups to which students belong and to learn how their cultures influence their learning and behavior. Teachers should also help students develop an understanding of their own cultural groups and acquire cultural identifications that are reflective and clarified cultural identifications, students

will hopefully acquire more positive attitudes toward their neighborhoods and communities.

(Banks, 1982, pp. 174–175)

A respect of cultural diversity is necessary to ensure that hegemonic forces do not take over our society to instill one singular cultural group in power. This has been the fate of many societies in the world and is the cause for costly civil strife. However, without a sense of amalgamation in a society, nothing ties the citizenry together and tribalism runs amok. For this reason, Banks (1982) argued for the importance of a national identity:

> As important as it is for the school to reflect cultural democracy and to respect and understand the students' cultures, it is also vitally important for all American youths to develop a reflective and clarified national identification and a strong commitment to American political ideals. An important role of the schools is to help socialize youths so that they develop the attitudes, values, and competencies needed to fully participate in the nation's civic life.

(p. 176)

Such values as equality, constitutional law, justice, and liberty may serve to unify a society with individuals who may have different historical experiences and contributions in our society. However, the typical pattern in civic education in democracies is to stress assimilation with little emphasis on diversification. Banks dedicated his career to fostering a strong curricular approach to multiculturalism that balanced the two forces.

Banks wrote prolifically on the theme of multicultural education and, over the years, conceived of a framework of dimensions of multicultural education that, when successfully implemented in the school curriculum, promises to yield a robust educational experience that better address the cultural needs of students. Figure 10.1 shows these dimensions of multiculturalism (Banks & McGee-Banks, 2009). The dimension of equity pedagogy means that a teacher uses instructional strategies that help facilitate academic success of students who may come from a marginalized population. This requires teachers to use research-based strategies that help foster student inquiry as opposed to something such as rote memorization and fact-recall types of activities. The dimension of knowledge construction refers to a teacher positioning students to critically reflect on how cultural perspectives influence the creation of knowledge. An example of this might be where a teacher positions students to analyze the gender and race constitution of a list of "classic" works of literature and juxtapose that with the relationship between gender, race, and cultural power that may have led to

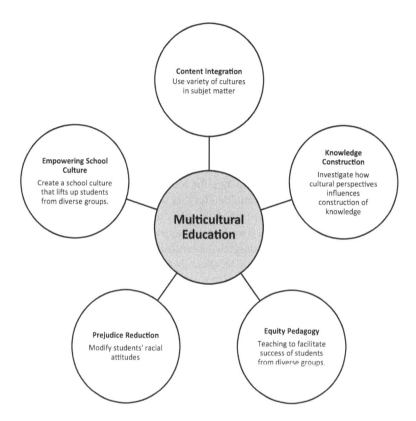

Figure 10.1 Dimensions of Multicultural Education
Source: Banks (2004)

such a list. Prejudice reduction requires the teacher to craft a curriculum that is intentional with modifying students' racial attitudes. This may come in the form of exposing students to perspectives from a variety of cultures and activities that require students to reflect on what types of attitudes help to uplift students typically marginalized from society and which ones perpetuate the marginalization. The dimension of empowering school culture involves students positioned to analyze the entire school organization and how it may better serve to uplift and empower students from all cultural backgrounds, not just those students from backgrounds that are typically privileged. Finally, the cultural dimension most foundational to any commitment to multicultural education is what Banks called content integration.

This involves teachers fairly representing examples from a variety of cultures into the subject matter they teach students. For instance, a social studies teacher should position students to examine such historical events as World War II from other peoples' perspectives such as the Chinese or perhaps use a diverse array of case study examples of active civic participation in an American Government course that may include members of the LGBTQ+ community, African American community, or perhaps citizens who are Jewish or Muslim who took action to defend their civil rights.

Banks' work on multicultural education provides direction for social studies teachers to better position their classroom practices to not only meet the cultural needs for each student but to also better serve a culturally pluralistic democracy. The challenge for social studies teachers remains to reflect all the dimensions of multicultural education. This is an especially daunting task in communities where hostility to multicultural education is prominent. Yet it is necessary work to perpetuate our democratic society.

The next section focuses on global education. Like multicultural education, global education requires teachers to expand students' perspectives beyond just their own individual interests and experiences.

Global Education

The need to learn about the world has always been a part of the tradition of social studies education. A look back at Harold Rugg's texts speak loudly to this fact. However, a concerted effort to imbue the social studies curriculum with a global perspective rose to prominence beginning in the 1980s with a significant gain in traction within the field in the 1990s. Global education gained some curricular steam with the rise of *globalization* that emerged with the decline and eventual fall of the Soviet Union. With the world no longer submerged in a Cold War rift between the separate aims of capitalist and communist societies, economic forces led to closer connection between countries. Regardless of the reason, *global education* gained prominence in the field of social studies education at this time.

In 1981, *Gene Gilliom* (b. 1932), a social studies educator at the Ohio State University, argued that the increasingly interdependent nature of our world required "an education designed to prepare citizens for effective participation in a global transnational society" (Gilliom, 1981, p. 169). Gilliom (1981) defined global education in this way:

> Definitions of global education abound, but in essence it can be thought of as those educational efforts designed to cultivate in young people a global perspective and to develop in them the knowledge, skills, and attitudes needed to live effectively in a world possessing limited natural resources

and characterized by ethnic diversity, cultural pluralism, and increasing interdependence. Although global education recognizes the importance of commonalities among mankind, it also is concerned with the differences among peoples and nations. A person with a global perspective recognizes that we are all members of a single species, enriched by diversity.

(p. 170)

Rather than suggesting an increase in more separate coursework on global issues, Gilliom and many other proponents of global education believed the best approach in this area is to infuse the curriculum with a global perspective. "The subject matter of global education permeates the total curriculum," Gilliom (1981) espoused that it (global education) "should be viewed as pervasive – a thread that runs throughout a student's entire school experience" (p. 170). Table 10.1 provides four different examples, in four separate classes, how a teacher in that class may seek to infuse a global perspective in their curriculum.

In 2016, the National Council for the Social Studies issued a position statement on global and international education. It emphasized a concern

Table 10.1 Examples of Infusing Global Perspectives (Gilliom, 1981)

Eighth-Grade American History	*Tenth-Grade Geography*	*Tenth-Grade Economics*	*Twelfth-Grade Sociology*
Teacher focuses on World War II and the internment of American citizens of Japanese descent. This includes a study of ethnocentrism and how stereotyping of individuals from a particular perspective can affect how people respond to international actions and policies.	Teacher focuses on international trade and has students analyze how local communities have global connections. Central to this analysis may be a survey of a local grocery to determine which items were imported and the economic and cultural implications of their findings.	Teacher focuses on causes and effects of labor unrest in the United States. In doing so, students are positioned to study labor/management relations in Japan, comparing/ contrasting their findings with what occurs in the United States. A local stationed executive of a Japanese firm may be invited to class to share their perspective on the issue.	Teacher focuses on families and supplements American-centric textbook by having students analyze family patterns in Greece, leading to the production of case studies of life in a Greek family.

that collective efforts to infuse global perspectives in the social studies curriculum had fallen and often resulted in "presenting a fragmentary view of the world" (NCSS, 2016). In the same spirit as Gene Gilliom from nearly 35 years earlier, the authors of the 2016 position statement stressed that an effective infusion of global education in the mainstream social studies curriculum should correlate with contemporary issues that may deal with change and interdependence in the hearts of human and natural systems. "For example," the position statement asserted, "a global perspective on a topic such as population change might lead to an examination of the impact of this change on environment quality and resource management." The position statement went on to suggest approaches teachers should use to engage students in global education. The following are some of those suggestions (NCSS, 2016):

- Use an interdisciplinary approach within and beyond social studies and make links to multicultural education.
- Emphasize interactive methodology, such as a model United Nations and cross-cultural simulations and role plays.
- Address global issues with an approach that promotes multiple perspectives and intellectual honesty and action.

These suggestions fit well with Gilliom's views on the infusion of global education and promise to create a synergistic teaching and learning experience that is relevant and meaningful to students. Regardless of the academic discipline a teacher may be responsible to teach, global education is an area, like multiculturalism, which should permeate all areas of students' educational experiences. In doing so, teachers are expanding students' understanding of the world and empowering them to play a responsible role in improving it.

Technology

Just as efforts toward multiculturalism and global education became woven in the fabric of what practitioners came to view as a strengthening of the social studies' commitment to democratic citizenship, a change came upon our society's cultural landscape that promised to alter the landscape of teaching and learning forever: the advent of *digital technology*. While technological change has always existed, digital technology is an innovation that is new in many ways. First, digital technologies are highly interactive and can exist in many forms. Personal computers, handheld devices, and software applications enable new opportunities for individuals to both create things on the Internet and explore and analyze an ever-expanding body of knowledge. Second, such digital technologies change at an increasingly rapid pace. This change results in a need for individuals to quickly adapt to new hardware and software despite feeling comfortable with previous versions of the technology. These new technologies affect how citizens interact with one another and how they learn. As a result, social studies teachers must nimbly adjust their classroom practice according to the changes brought forth from new digital technologies.

In 1997, *Peter Martorella* (b. 1939), a professor of social studies education at North Carolina State University, addressed how the field should address technological change. Calling technology a "sleeping giant," Martorella (1997) asserted that despite the changes technology brought to society and schools where "the visual has achieved supremacy over the written or spoken word," the social studies curriculum has been little affected by this change (p. 511). He went on to advocate for social studies educators to prioritize research and dialogue on technology use in the classroom.

Since Martorella's plea for progress in technology infusion in social studies education, progress has been made on this front. Many scholars in the field have studied and written extensively about the use of various digital technologies in the social studies classroom. Some, for instance, have focused on historical inquiry (e.g., Saye & Brush, 2009; Friedman, 2009) while others (e.g., Humphries & Washington, 2014; Hostetler et al., 2014) have focused on areas such as democratic dialogue and deliberation in online spaces. One area of research and practice I am particularly close to is that of *desktop documentary making* in history classroom. A desktop documentary is simply a film composed on a desktop (or laptop or handheld device) where students collect web-based imagery and craft a historical narrative that weaves together this imagery with various filmmaking techniques (see Schul, 2014a, for an elaboration on desktop documentary making). My experience with teachers and students alike is that desktop documentary making enables students to engage in historical inquiry at an individual level (Schul, 2012a, 2014b) and, through viewing one another's documentary as part of the class assignment, enables students to engage in historical discourse with one another as well as to help foster a lively intellectual and caring community in the classroom (Fehn & Schul, 2014; Schul, 2012b).

One helpful framework that enabled further research (including much of my own) and, in turn, propelled enhanced classroom practice regarding technology use is *Technological Pedagogical Content Knowledge* (TPACK). The TPACK framework was conceived by two educational researchers from Michigan State University named *Punya Mishra* and *Matthew Koehler*. They started with a framework first conceived by Stanford's *Lee Shulman* (b. 1938) called *Pedagogical Content Knowledge* (PCK) that combined a teacher's knowledge of pedagogy with their knowledge of subject matter to put forth what is now understood to be a teacher's professional knowledge in that it pinpoints a teacher's ability to transform subject matter for student comprehension and understanding. According to Shulman (1986), PCK "includes an understanding of what makes the learning of specific topics easy or difficult" and "knowledge of the strategies most likely to be fruitful in reorganizing the understanding of learners" (p. 9). This framework became a dynamic path for researchers to take to examine and improve upon the relationship between teacher practice and student learning. As a case in point, Sam Wineburg used this framework to catapult his robust work on history teaching and learning over the past quarter of a century. Mishra and Koehler (2006) created a new dynamic with Shulman's framework by adding technological knowledge to it. Figure 10.2 displays a visual of what Mishra and Koehler's framework looks like.

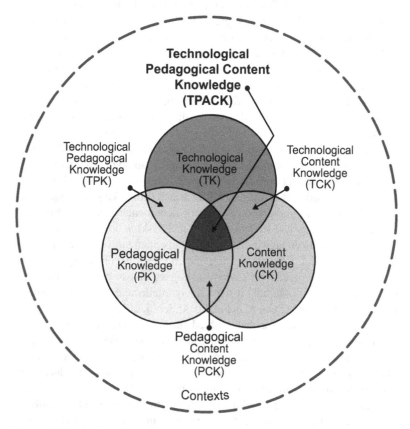

Figure 10.2 TPACK Model

As shown in this figure, the TPACK framework enables for examination of a teacher's pedagogical knowledge (P), content knowledge (C), and technological knowledge (T). The mergence of these three components enables an analysis of a teacher's ability to use technology (T) to teach students (P) how to comprehend and understand subject matter (C). The mergence of these three features makes up a teacher's unique Technological Pedagogical Content Knowledge. Additionally, the TPACK framework includes a feature where researchers may also pinpoint each component in isolation from one another or paired with one another in different ways: Pedagogical Content Knowledge (PCK), Technological Content Knowledge (TCK), and Technological Pedagogical Knowledge (TPK). While PCK has already been addressed, TCK consists of a teacher's knowledge of certain technologies and how they may help with the teaching of areas of subject matter. Technological Pedagogical Knowledge (TPK) consists of a teacher's knowledge of how a technology may be used beyond its conventional use (i.e., data entry or entertainment) and used instead to improve upon teaching and learning. For instance, the software for desktop documentary making was originally targeted for social productions such as weddings or graduation ceremonies – not development of historical narratives.

The key contribution of the TPACK framework is that it ties together technology use with student learning. I once conducted a small research study on middle and secondary social studies teachers and teacher candidates that examined the teachers' perceptions of desktop documentary making (Schul, 2017). Although the study was small in scope, it revealed a truth that illustrates the effectiveness of the TPACK model. While some of the teachers envisioned using desktop documentary making in ways that they believed would enhance students' historical understanding and imagination, some perceived that the most attractive feature of desktop documentary making was that it merely provided a technological experience for students. In sum, the former teachers had a more refined TPACK in that they were able to envision how a digital technology enhanced student learning of subject matter. However, the latter teachers indicated that their TPACK was not as refined in that they were just able to see their knowledge of the technology (TK) as opposed to how it transformed student learning. The difference between the two teacher sets is that, to use Martorella's analogy, one has the giant of technological change awake in their classroom, whereas others have kept this giant in its slumber. Technological Pedagogical Content Knowledge helps researchers and practitioners to better see the dynamic of both classrooms and, in turn, potentially awaken the sleeping giant in all classrooms.

Summary

It is the aim of social studies educators to develop citizens who are equipped to be effectively engaged in their society. Three areas that the field of social studies education has developed and refined in years leading up to, and the two decades since, the dawn of the twenty-first century is multiculturalism, global education, and technology. Multiculturalism involves a broad attempt to reshape the curriculum and curricular practices that better reflect the cultural differences that make up the country's pluralistic democracy. Global education consists of a curriculum that resonates with the global interconnectedness that is foundational to modern society. Technology encompasses the effective integration of digital technologies in classroom practices that improve teaching and learning of subject matter. Each of these three areas should be infused in the social studies curriculum, regardless of the subject matter being taught. In this sense, infusing these areas in all social studies courses promises to invigorate relevancy and modernity in students' lives. The final aim and goal in doing so is to include and empower students to be fully prepared and involved in the American democratic project going forward in the twenty-first century.

Reflective Exercises

1. Reflect upon your own experience as a student in social studies classes. Were they infused with multiculturalism, global education, and technology? Explain.
2. Look at Figure 10.1. Pick a school of your choice that you're familiar with. How does that school address each of the five areas of multicultural education? Explain your answer for each of those areas.
3. How may a social studies teacher teach a lesson on the American Civil War in such a way that infuses global education?
4. What are some challenges teachers may face when integrating digital technologies? How may a teacher effectively overcome those challenges?

References

Banks, J. A. (2002). Cultural democracy, citizenship education, and the American dream. In M. A. Previte & J. J. Sheehan (Eds.), *The NCSS presidential addresses, 1970–2000: Perspectives on the social studies* (pp. 167–188). National Council for the Social Studies. (Original work published 1982)

Banks, J. A. (2004). Multicultural education: Historical development, dimensions, and practice. In J. A. Banks & C. A. M. Banks (Eds.), *Handbook of research on multicultural education* (2nd ed., pp. 3–29). San Francisco: Jossey-Bass.

Clabough, J., & Clyde, R. G. (2021). NCSS: An advocate for diverse voices. *Social Education, 85*(4), 248–252.

Fehn, B., & Schul, J. E. (2014). Selective appropriation and historical documentary making in a special education classroom. *Social Studies Research & Practice*, *9*(2).

Friedman, A. (2009). The effect of teachers' conceptions of student abilities and historical thinking on digital primary source use. In J. K. Lee & A. Friedman (Eds.), *Research on technology in social studies education* (pp. 189–204). Information Age Publishing.

Gilliom, M. E. (1981). Global education and the social studies. *Theory into Practice*, 169–173.

Hostetler, A. L., Crowe, A. R., & Ashkettle, B. (2014). Talking and listening across difference: Teaching democratic citizenship in online discussion spaces. In W. Russell (Ed.), *Digital social studies* (pp. 321–344). Information Age Publishing.

Humphries, E. K., & Washington, E. Y. (2014). Mashing Socrates and Zuckerberg: Discussing social issues with social technologies. In W. Russell (Ed.), *Digital social studies* (pp. 303–320). Information Age Publishing.

Martorella, P. H. (1997). Technology and the social studies—or: Which way to the sleeping giant? *Theory & Research in Social Education*, *25*(4), 511–514.

Mishra, P., & Koehler, M. J. (2006). Technological pedagogical content knowledge: A framework for teacher knowledge. *Teachers college record*, *108*(6), 1017–1054.

National Council for the Social Studies (NCSS). (2016). *Global and international education*. www.socialstudies.org/position-statements/global-and-international-education-social-studies.

Saye, J. W., & Brush, T. A. (2009). Using the affordances of technology to develop teacher expertise in historical inquiry. In J. K. Lee & A. Friedman (Eds.), *Research on technology in social studies education* (pp. 19–38). Information Age Publishing.

Schul, J. E. (2012a). Compositional encounters: Evolvement of secondary students' narratives while making historical desktop documentaries. *Journal of Social Studies Research*, *36*(3), 219–244.

Schul, J. E. (2012b). Toward a community of learners: Integrating desktop documentary making in a general secondary history classroom. *International Journal of Technology in Teaching & Learning*, *8*(1).

Schul, J. E. (2014a). Film pedagogy in the history classroom: Desktop documentary-making skills for history teachers and students. *The Social Studies*, *105*(1), 15–22.

Schul, J. E. (2014b). Emotional evocation and desktop documentary making: Secondary students' motivations while composing historical documentaries. In W. Russell (Ed.), *Digital social studies* (pp. 439–465). Information Age Publishing.

Schul, J. E. (2017). Technology for its own sake: Teachers' purpose and practice with desktop documentary making. *Social Studies Education Review*, *6*(1), 43–62.

Shulman, L. (1986). Those who understand: Knowledge growth in teaching. *Educational Researcher*, *15*(2), 4–14.

Afterword

If destruction be our lot we must ourselves be its author and finisher. As a nation of freemen we must live through all time or die by suicide.

— Abraham Lincoln (1838)

On January 6, 2021, a mob, numbering in the thousands, invaded the United States Capitol building in a quest to stop the certification of the 2020 presidential election and simultaneously seek out and execute specific individuals they deemed to be enemies. Atop their list was the vice president of the United States and the speaker of the House of Representatives. Cloaked in a facade of patriotic zeal, these seditionists crushed police barricades and assailed officers who stood in their way. Rage united them, as their thoughts and motives were clouded by a thick fog of conspiracy theories, lies, and cultural tribalism.

This invasion did not come from an enemy abroad. Instead, it came from within. These were American citizens, and they were urged on, not by a despot from afar but by the president of the United States as a way for him to remain in power after losing a fair and legal election. In many ways, the tragic events of what has come to be known as the January sixth insurrection could be foreseen. That man who was president of the United States had a long history of lies and did not like to be publicly embarrassed or seen as a loser. When elected in 2016, he was a known provocateur whose long success as a reality TV star empowered him to succeed in a political climate already decimated by a partisan-filled ecosystem that disregarded evidence and thrived off enmity within the citizenry.

While those of us who care about democracy should be concerned about future actions of that man who was president, it is the citizenry who should hold our greatest concern. In the aftermath of the January sixth insurrection, attempts arose across the national landscape to whitewash it from our collective memory. It didn't take long for those entrenched in the camp of the president to make excuses, downplay, or to otherwise rationalize away any bearing of responsibility they or even the president might have for the horrific events of that day. Even political leaders from the president's political party, who initially denounced the president, found themselves in fear of their own constituency for doing so. As a result, the leaders once again found a way to align themselves back with that president. Every community or neighborhood in the country has at least a pocket of people who saw little to nothing wrong with the events of January sixth. This would be unfathomable earlier in the country's history. To make matters worse, we are lulled away from even noticing such societal decay as we slouch toward authoritarianism. The newest shows and movies continue to stream, our favorite sports teams continue to win or break our hearts, and social media engrosses our insatiable thirst for knowing others' business or sharing our own.

Is the future as bleak for democracy as it appears? The past may very well serve as the lone blueprint for our future. We did have a similar time when authoritarianism posed a serious threat to democracy across the Western world. The years leading up to the Second World War contained classic examples of authoritarian threats and conquest. But world war need not be our destiny. We should heed words of individuals from that dark time who espoused a vision for a better, brighter, more democratic future. One such individual just may be the most significant (and the most underrated) figure in the history of social studies education: Boyd Bode.

Bode was a philosopher extraordinaire at the Ohio State University in the early to mid-twentieth century. He is seldom acknowledged today, and yet he was the prophet for democratic education that we should come to intimately know at this present moment for three key reasons. First, he clearly articulated what a democracy should look like. Rather than a mere political system that enables rule of the majority, he viewed democracy as a distinctive way of life. This way of life consists of a distinctive style of interpersonal relationships that value mutual tolerance and advocacy for others. It also consists of a distinctive type of intrapersonal dispositional commitment to the greater good of society (Bode, 1939). Second, he believed the public school was necessary for the perpetuation of democratic life and was where "democracy becomes conscious of itself" (Bode, 1939, p. 95). If democracy consisted of a distinctive way of life, then "it must have also a distinctive educational system" (Bode, 1938, p. 26). Finally, as a teacher of teacher educators, Bode invested in his own students as the caretakers of democracy. He was the mentor of many great teacher educators, but as far as social studies education is concerned, his investment in Alan Griffin was central to the development of the field.

Is Bode's brand of democracy as a distinctive way of life possible for us in our current situation? I think so. Imagine if our youth today grew up:

- having the skill set to reflectively think prior to impulsively accepting information shared with them on social media platforms.
- with the kind of historical knowledge that helped them make better sense of their world today.
- with a commitment to making evidentiary stances on public policy issues devoid of partisanship.
- morally healthy with a recognition of their relationship as individuals to the greater society.
- striving to be caring, loving, and lovable people.
- less vulnerable to succumbing to their community's closed areas and more willing to publicly address and deliberate about them.

These visions of the future may seem far-fetched, but I firmly believe this future is within our grasp. Good schools with good teachers can achieve good things.

Bode reminded us that we live amidst a drama of cosmic proportions. Democracy or authoritarianism, which will it be? The primary actors on this stage are none other than the social studies teachers who populate classrooms across democracies throughout the world. They are our key figures commissioned with the cosmic charge of democratizing the public.

References

Bode, B. H. (1938). *Progressive education at the crossroads*. Newson & Company.

Bode, B. H. (1939). *Democracy as a way of life*. Macmillan.

Index